THE SUITORS OF YVONNE

CONTENTS

CHAPTER I

OF HOW A BOY DRANK TOO MUCH WINE, AND WHAT CAME OF IT

Andrea de Mancini sprawled, ingloriously drunk, upon the floor. His legs were thrust under the table, and his head rested against the chair from which he had slipped; his long black hair was tossed and dishevelled; his handsome, boyish face flushed and garbed in the vacant expression of idiocy.

"I beg a thousand pardons, M. de Luynes," quoth he in the thick, monotonous voice of a man whose brain but ill controls his tongue,—"I beg a thousand pardons for the unseemly poverty of our repast. 'T is no fault of mine. My Lord Cardinal keeps a most unworthy table for me. Faugh! Uncle Giulio is a Hebrew—if not by birth, by instinct. He carries his purse-strings in a knot which it would break his heart to unfasten. But there! some day my Lord Cardinal will go to heaven—to the lap of Abraham. I shall be rich then, vastly rich, and I shall bid you to a banquet worthy of your most noble blood. The Cardinal's health—perdition have him for the niggardliest rogue unhung!"

I pushed back my chair and rose. The conversation was taking a turn that was too unhealthy to be pursued within the walls of the Palais Mazarin, where there existed, albeit the law books made no reference to it, the heinous crime of lèse-Eminence—a crime for which more men had been broken than it pleases me to dwell on.

"Your table, Master Andrea, needs no apology," I answered carelessly. "Your wine, for instance, is beyond praise."

"Ah, yes! The wine! But, ciel! Monsieur," he ejaculated, for a moment opening wide his heavy eyelids, "do you believe 't was Mazarin provided it? Pooh! 'T was a present made me by M. de la Motte, who seeks my interest with my Lord Cardinal to obtain for him an appointment in his Eminence's household, and thus thinks to earn my good will. He's a pestilent creature, this la Motte," he added, with a hiccough,—"a pestilent creature; but, Sangdieu! his wine is good, and I'll speak to my uncle. Help me up, De Luynes. Help me up, I say; I would drink the health of this provider of wines."

I hurried forward, but he had struggled up unaided, and stood swaying with one hand on the table and the other on the back of his chair. In vain did I remonstrate with him that already he had drunk overmuch.

"'T is a lie!" he shouted. "May not a gentleman sit upon the floor from choice?"

To emphasise his protestation he imprudently withdrew his hand from the chair and struck at the air with his open palm. That gesture cost him his balance. He staggered, toppled backward, and clutched madly at the tablecloth as he fell, dragging glasses, bottles, dishes, tapers, and a score of other things besides, with a deafening crash on to the floor.

Then, as I stood aghast and alarmed, wondering who might have overheard the thunder of his fall, the fool sat up amidst the ruins, and filled the room with his shrieks of drunken laughter.

"Silence, boy!" I thundered, springing towards him. "Silence! or we shall have the whole house about our ears."

And truly were my fears well grounded, for, before I could assist him to rise, I heard the door behind me open. Apprehensively I turned, and sickened to see that that which I had dreaded most was come to pass. A tall, imposing figure in scarlet robes stood erect and scowling on the threshold, and behind him his valet, Bernouin, bearing a lighted taper.

Mancini's laugh faded into a tremulous cackle, then died out, and with gaping mouth and glassy eyes he sat there staring at his uncle.

Thus we stayed in silence while a man might count mayhap a dozen; then the Cardinal's voice rang harsh and full of anger.

"'T is thus that you fulfil your trust, M. de Luynes!" he said.

"Your Eminence—" I began, scarce knowing what I should say, when he cut me short.

"I will deal with you presently and elsewhere." He stepped up to Andrea, and surveyed him for a moment in disgust. "Get up, sir!" he commanded. "Get up!"

The lad sought to obey him with an alacrity that merited a kinder fate. Had he been in less haste perchance he had been more successful. As it was, he had got no farther than his knees when his right leg slid from under him, and he fell prone among the shattered tableware, mumbling curses and apologies in a breath.

Mazarin stood gazing at him with an eye that was eloquent in scorn, then bending down he spoke quickly to him in Italian. What he said I know not, being ignorant of their mother tongue; but from the fierceness of his utterance I'll wager my soul 't was nothing sweet to listen to. When he had done with him, he turned to his valet.

"Bernouin," said he, "summon M. de Mancini's servant and assist him to get my nephew to bed. M. de Luynes, be good enough to take Bernouin's taper and light me back to my apartments."

Unsavoury as was the task, I had no choice but to obey, and to stalk on in front of him, candle in hand, like an acolyte at Notre Dame, and in my heart the profound conviction that I was about to have a bad quarter of an hour with his Eminence. Nor was I wrong; for no sooner had we reached his cabinet and the door had been closed than he turned upon me the full measure of his wrath.

"You miserable fool!" he snarled. "Did you think to trifle with the trust which in a misguided moment I placed in you? Think you that, when a week ago I saved you from starvation to clothe and feed you and give you a lieutenancy in my guards, I should endure so foul an abuse as this? Think you that I entrusted M. de Mancini's training in arms to you so that you might lead him into the dissolute habits which have dragged you down to what you are—to what you were before I rescued you—to what you will be tomorrow when I shall have again abandoned you?"

"Hear me, your Eminence!" I cried indignantly. "'T is no fault of mine. Some fool hath sent M. de Mancini a basket of wine and—"

"And you showed him how to abuse it," he broke in harshly. "You have taught the boy to become a sot; in time, were he to remain under your guidance, I make no doubt but that he would become a gamester and a duellist as well. I was mad, perchance, to give him into your care; but I have the good fortune to be still in time, before the mischief has sunk farther, to withdraw him from it, and to cast you back into the kennel from which I picked you."

"Your Eminence does not mean—"

"As God lives I do!" he cried. "You shall quit the Palais Royal this very night, M. de Luynes, and if ever I find you unbidden within half a mile of it, I will do that which out of a misguided sense of compassion I do not do now—I will have you flung into an oubliette of the Bastille, where better men than you have rotted before today. Per Dio! do you think that I am to be fooled by such a thing as you?"

"Does your Eminence dismiss me?" I cried aghast, and scarce crediting that such was indeed the extreme measure upon which he had determined.

"Have I not been plain enough?" he answered with a snarl.

I realised to the full my unenviable position, and with the realisation of it there overcame me the recklessness of him who has played his last stake at the tables and lost. That recklessness it was that caused me to shrug my shoulders with a laugh. I was a soldier of fortune—or should I say a soldier of misfortune?—as rich in vice as I was poor in virtue; a man who lived by the steel and parried the blows that came as best he might, or parried them not at all—but never quailed.

"As your Eminence pleases," I answered coolly, "albeit methinks that for one who has shed his blood for France as freely as I have done, a little clemency were not unfitting."

He raised his eyebrows, and his lips curled in a malicious sneer.

"You come of a family, M. de Luynes," he said slowly, "that is famed for having shed the blood of others for France more freely than its own. You are, I believe, the nephew of Albert de Luynes. Do you forget the Marshal d'Ancre?"

I felt the blood of anger hot in my face as I made haste to answer him:

"There are many of us, Monseigneur, who have cause to blush for the families they spring from—more cause, mayhap, than hath Gaston de Luynes."

In my words perchance there was no offensive meaning, but in my tone and in the look which I bent upon the Cardinal there was that which told him that I alluded to his own obscure and dubious origin. He grew livid, and for a moment methought he would have struck me: had he done so, then, indeed, the history of Europe would have been other than it is today! He restrained himself, however, and drawing himself to the full height of his majestic figure he extended his arm towards the door.

"Go," he said, in a voice that passion rendered hoarse. "Go, Monsieur. Go quickly, while my clemency endures. Go before I summon the guard and deal with you as your temerity deserves."

I bowed—not without a taint of mockery, for I cared little what might follow; then, with head erect and the firm tread of defiance, I stalked out of his apartment, along the corridor, down the great staircase, across the courtyard, past the guard,—which, ignorant of my disgrace, saluted me,—and out into the street.

Then at last my head sank forward on my breast, and deep in thought I wended my way home, oblivious of all around me, even the chill bite of the February wind.

In my mind I reviewed my wasted life, with the fleeting pleasures and the enduring sorrows that it had brought me—or that I had drawn from it. The Cardinal said no more than truth when he spoke of having saved me from starvation. A week ago that was indeed what he had done. He had taken pity on Gaston de Luynes, the nephew of that famous Albert de Luynes who had been Constable of France in the early days of the late king's reign; he had made me lieutenant of his guards and maître d'armes to his nephews Andrea and Paolo de Mancini because he knew that a better blade than mine could not be found in France, and because he thought it well to have such swords as mine about him.

A little week ago life had been replete with fresh promises, the gates of the road to fame (and perchance fortune) had been opened to me anew, and now—before I had fairly passed that gate I had been thrust rudely back, and it had been slammed in my face because it pleased a fool to become a sot whilst in my company.

There is a subtle poetry in the contemplation of ruin. With ruin itself, howbeit, there comes a prosaic dispelling of all idle dreams—a hard, a grim, a vile reality.

Ruin! 'T is an ugly word. A fitting one to carve upon the tombstone of a reckless, godless, dissolute life such as mine had been.

Back, Gaston de Luynes! back, to the kennel whence the Cardinal's hand did for a moment pluck you; back, from the morning of hope to the night of despair; back, to choose between starvation and the earning of a pauper's fee as a master of fence!

CHAPTER II

THE FRUIT OF INDISCRETION

Despite the dejection to which I had become a prey, I slept no less soundly that night than was my wont, and indeed it was not until late next morning when someone knocked at my door that I awakened.

I sat up in bed, and my first thought as I looked round the handsome room—which I had rented a week ago upon receiving the lieutenancy in the Cardinal's guards—was for the position that I had lost and of the need that there would be ere long to seek a lodging more humble and better suited to my straitened circumstances. It was not without regret that such a thought came to me, for my tastes had never been modest, and the house was a fine one, situated in the Rue St. Antoine at a hundred paces or so from the Jesuit convent.

I had no time, however, to indulge the sorry mood that threatened to beset me, for the knocking at my chamber door continued, until at length I answered it with a command to enter.

It was my servant Michelot, a grizzled veteran of huge frame and strength, who had fought beside me at Rocroi, and who had thereafter become so enamoured of my person—for some trivial service he swore I had rendered him—that he had attached himself to me and my luckless fortunes.

He came to inform me that M. de Mancini was below and craved immediate speech with me. He had scarce done speaking, however, when Andrea himself, having doubtless grown tired of waiting, appeared in the doorway. He wore a sickly look, the result of his last night's debauch; but, more than that, there was stamped upon his face a look of latent passion which made me think at first that he was come to upbraid me.

"Ah, still abed, Luynes?" was his greeting as he came forward.

His cloak was wet and his boots splashed, which told me both that he had come afoot and that it rained.

"There are no duties that bid me rise," I answered sourly.

He frowned at that, then, divesting himself of his cloak, he gave it to Michelot, who, at a sign from me, withdrew. No sooner was the door closed than the boy's whole manner changed. The simmering passion of which I had detected signs welled up and seemed to choke him as he poured forth the story that he had come to tell.

"I have been insulted," he gasped. "Grossly insulted by a vile creature of Monsieur d'Orleans's household. An hour ago in the ante-chamber at the Palais Royal I was spoken of in my hearing as the besotted nephew of the Italian adventurer."

I sat up in bed tingling with excitement at the developments which already I saw arising from his last night's imprudence.

"Calmly, Andrea," I begged of him, "tell me calmly."

"Mortdieu! How can I be calm? Ough! The thought of it chokes me. I was a fool last night—a sot. For that, perchance, men have some right to censure me. But, Sangdieu! that a ruffler of the stamp of Eugène de Canaples should speak of it—should call me the nephew of an Italian adventurer, should draw down upon me the cynical smile of a crowd of courtly apes—pah! I am sick at the memory of it!"

"Did you answer him?"

"Pardieu! I should be worthy of the title he bestowed upon me had I not done so. Oh, I answered him—not in words. I threw my hat in his face."

"That was a passing eloquent reply!"

"So eloquent that it left him speechless with amazement. He thought to bully with impunity, and see me slink into hiding like a whipped dog, terrified by his blustering tongue and dangerous reputation. But there!" he broke off, "a meeting has been arranged for four o'clock at St. Germain."

"A meeting!" I exclaimed.

"What else? Do you think the affront left any alternative?"

"But—"

"Yes, yes, I know," he interrupted, tossing his head. "I am going to be killed. Verville has sworn that there shall be one less of the Italian brood. That is why I have come to you, Luynes—to ask you to be my second. I don't deserve it, perhaps. In my folly last night I did you an ill turn. I unwittingly caused you to be stripped of your commission. But if I were on my death-bed now, and begged a favour of you, you would not refuse it. And what difference is there 'twixt me and one who is on his death-bed? Am I not about to die?"

"Peste! I hope not," I made answer with more lightness than I felt. "But I'll stand by you with all my heart, Andrea."

"And you'll avenge me?" he cried savagely, his Southern blood a-boiling. "You'll not let him leave the ground alive?"

"Not unless my opponent commits the indiscretion of killing me first. Who seconds M. de Canaples?"

"The Marquis de St. Auban and M. de Montmédy."

"And who is the third in our party?"

"I have none. I thought that perhaps you had a friend."

"I! A friend?" I laughed bitterly. "Pshaw, Andrea! beggars have no friends. But stay; find Stanislas de Gouville. There is no better blade in Paris. If he will join us in this frolic, and you can hold off Canaples until either St. Auban or Montmédy is disposed of, we may yet leave the three of them on the field of battle. Courage, Andrea! Dum spiramus, speramus."

My words seemed to cheer him, and when presently he left me to seek out the redoubtable Gouville, the poor lad's face was brighter by far than when he had entered my room.

Down in my heart, however, I was less hopeful than I had led him to believe, and as I dressed after he had gone, 't was not without some uneasiness that I turned the matter over in my mind. I had, during the short period of our association, grown fond of Andrea de Mancini. Indeed the wonted sweetness of the lad's temper, and the gentleness of his disposition, were such as to breed affection in all who came in contact with him. In a way, too, methought he had grown fond of me, and I had known so few friends in life,—truth to tell I fear me that I had few of the qualities that engender friendship,—that I was naturally prone to appreciate a gift that from its rareness became doubly valuable.

Hence was it that I trembled for the boy. He had shown aptitude with the foils, and derived great profit from my tuition, yet he was too raw by far to be pitted against so cunning a swordsman as Canaples.

I had but finished dressing when a coach rumbled down the street and halted by my door. Naturally I supposed that someone came to visit Coupri, the apothecary,—to whom belonged this house in which I had my lodging,—and did not give the matter a second thought until Michelot rushed in, with eyes wide open, to announce that his Eminence, Cardinal Mazarin, commanded my presence in the adjoining room.

Amazed and deeply marvelling what so extraordinary a visit might portend, I hastened to wait upon his Eminence.

I found him standing by the window, and received from him a greeting that was passing curt and cavalier.

"Has M. de Mancini been here?" he inquired peremptorily, disregarding the chair I offered him.

"He has but left me, Monseigneur."

"Then you know, sir, of the harvest which he has already reaped from the indiscretion into which you led him last night?"

"If Monseigneur alludes to the affront put upon M. de Mancini touching his last night's indiscretion, by a bully of the Court, I am informed of it."

"Pish, Monsieur! I do not follow your fine distinctions—possibly this is due to my imperfect knowledge of the language of France, possibly to your own imperfect acquaintance with the language of truth."

"Monseigneur!"

"Faugh!" he cried, half scornfully, half peevishly. "I came not here to talk of you, but of my nephew. Why did he visit you?"

"To do me the honour of asking me to second him at St. Germain this evening."

"And so you think that this duel is to be fought?—that my nephew is to be murdered?"

"We will endeavour to prevent his being—as your Eminence daintily puts it—murdered. But for the rest, the duel, methinks, cannot be avoided."

"Cannot!" he blazed. "Do you say cannot, M. de Luynes? Mark me well, sir: I will use no dissimulation with you. My position in France is already a sufficiently difficult one. Already we are threatened with a second Fronde. It needs but such events as these to bring my family into prominence and make it the butt for the ridicule that malcontents but wait an opportunity to slur it with. This affair of Andrea's will lend itself to a score or so of lampoons and pasquinades, all of which will cast an injurious reflection upon my person and position. That, Monsieur, is, methinks, sufficient evil to suffer at your hands. The late Cardinal would have had you broken on the wheel for less. I have gone no farther than to dismiss you from my service—a clemency for which you should be grateful. But I shall not suffer that, in addition to the harm already done, Andrea shall be murdered by Canaples."

"I shall do my best to render him assistance."

"You still misapprehend me. This duel, sir, must not take place."

I shrugged my shoulders.

"How does your Eminence propose to frustrate it? Will you arrest Canaples?"

"Upon what plea, Monsieur? Think you I am anxious to have the whole of Paris howling in my ears?"

"Then possibly it is your good purpose to enforce the late king's edict against duelling, and send your guards to St. Germain to arrest the men before they engage?"

"Benone!" he sneered. "And what will Paris say if I now enforce a law that for ten years has been disregarded? That I feared for my nephew's skin and took this means of saving him. A pretty story to have on Paris's lips, would it not be?"

"Indeed, Monseigneur, you are right, but I doubt me the duel will needs be fought."

"Have I not already said that it shall not be fought?"

Again I shrugged my shoulders. Mazarin grew tiresome with his repetitions.

"How can it be avoided, your Eminence?"

"Ah, Monsieur, that is your affair."

"My affair?"

"Assuredly. 'T was through your evil agency he was dragged into this business, and through your agency he must be extricated from it."

"Your Eminence jests!"

"Undoubtedly,—'t is a jesting matter," he answered with terrible irony. "Oh, I jest! Per Dio! yes. But I'll carry my jest so far as to have you hanged if this duel be fought—aye, whether my nephew suffers hurt or not. Now, sir, you know what fate awaits you; fight it—turn it aside—I have shown you the way. The door, M. de Luynes."

CHAPTER III

THE FIGHT IN THE HORSE-MARKET

I let him go without a word. There was that in his voice, in his eye, and in the gesture wherewith he bade me hold the door for him, that cleared my mind of any doubts touching the irrevocable character of his determination. To plead was never an accomplishment of mine; to argue, I saw, would be to waste the Cardinal's time to no purpose.

And so I let him go,—and my curse with him,—and from my window I watched his coach drive away in the drizzling rain, scattering the crowd of awe-stricken loiterers who had collected at the rumour of his presence.

With a fervent prayer that his patron saint, the devil, might see fit to overset his coach and break his neck before he reached the Palace, I turned from the window, and called Michelot.

He was quick to answer my summons, bringing me the frugal measure of bread and wine wherewith it was my custom to break my fast. Then, whilst I munched my crust, I strode to and fro in the little chamber and exercised my wits to their utmost for a solution to the puzzle his Eminence had set me.

One solution there was, and an easy one—flight. But I had promised Andrea de Mancini that I would stand beside him at St. Germain; there was a slender chance of saving him if I went, whilst, if I stayed away, there would be nothing left for his Eminence to do but to offer up prayers for the rest of his nephew's soul.

Another idea I had, but it was desperate—and yet, so persistently did my thoughts revert to it that in the end I determined to accept it.

I drank a cup of Armagnac, cheered myself with an oath or two, and again I called Michelot. When he came, I asked him if he were acquainted with M. de Canaples, to which he replied that he was, having seen the gentleman in my company.

"Then," I said, "you will repair to M. de Canaples's lodging in the Rue des Gesvres, and ascertain discreetly whether he be at home. If he is, you will watch the house until he comes forth, then follow him, and bring me word thereafter where he is to be found. Should he be already abroad before you reach the Rue des Gesvres, endeavour to ascertain whither he has gone, and return forthwith. But be discreet, Michelot. You understand?"

He assured me that he did, and left me to nurse my unpleasant thoughts for half an hour, returning at the end of that time with the information that M. de Canaples was seated at dinner in the "Auberge du Soleil."

Naught could have been more attuned to my purpose, and straightway I drew on my boots, girt on my sword, and taking my hat and cloak, I sallied out into the rain, and wended my way at a sharp pace towards the Rue St. Honoré.

One o'clock was striking as I crossed the threshold of the "Soleil" and flung my dripping cloak to the first servant I chanced upon.

I glanced round the well-filled room, and at one of the tables I espied my quarry in company with St. Auban and Montmédy—the very gentlemen who were to fight beside him that evening—and one Vilmorin, as arrant a coxcomb and poltroon as could be found in France. With my beaver cocked at the back of my head, and a general bearing that for aggressiveness would be hard to surpass, I strode up to their table, and stood for a moment surveying them with an insolent stare that made them pause in their conversation. They raised their noble heads and bestowed upon me a look of haughty and disdainful wonder,—such a look as one might bestow upon a misbehaving lackey,—all save Vilmorin, who, with a coward's keen nose for danger, turned slightly pale and fidgeted in his chair. I was well known to all of them, but my attitude forbade all greeting.

"Has M. de Luynes lost anything?" St. Auban inquired icily.

"His wits, mayhap," quoth Canaples with a contemptuous shrug.

He was a tall, powerfully built man, this Canaples, with a swart, cruel face that was nevertheless not ill-favoured, and a profusion of black hair.

"There is a temerity in M. de Canaples's rejoinder that I had not looked for," I said banteringly.

Canaples's brow was puckered in a frown.

"Ha! And why not, Monsieur?"

"Why not? Because it is not to be expected that one who fastens quarrels upon schoolboys would evince the courage to beard Gaston de Luynes."

"Monsieur!" the four of them cried in chorus, so loudly that the hum of voices in the tavern became hushed, and all eyes were turned in our direction.

"M. de Canaples," I said calmly, "permit me to say that I can find no more fitting expression for the contempt I hold you in than this."

As I spoke I seized a corner of the tablecloth, and with a sudden tug I swept it, with all it held, on to the floor.

Dame! what a scene there was! In an instant the four of them were on their feet,—as were half the occupants of the room, besides,—whilst poor Vilmorin, who stood trembling like a maid who for the first time hears words of love, raised his quavering voice to cry soothingly, "Messieurs, Messieurs!"

Canaples was livid with passion, but otherwise the calmest in that room, saving perhaps myself. With a gesture he restrained Montmédy and St. Auban.

"I shall be happy to give Master de Luynes all the proof of my courage that he may desire, and more, I warrant, than he will relish."

"Bravely answered!" I cried, with an approving nod and a beaming smile. "Be good enough to lead the way to a convenient spot."

"I have other business at the moment," he answered calmly. "Let us say tomorrow at—"

"Faugh!" I broke in scornfully. "I knew it! Confess, Monsieur, that you dare not light me now lest you should be unable to keep your appointments for this evening."

"Mille diables!" exclaimed St. Auban, "this insolence passes all bounds."

"Each man in his turn if you please, gentlemen," I replied. "My present affair is with M. de Canaples."

There was a hot answer burning on St. Auban's lips, but Canaples was beforehand with him.

"Par la mort Dieu!" he cried; "you go too far, sir, with your 'dare' and 'dare not.' Is a broken gamester, a penniless adventurer, to tell Eugène de Canaples what he dares? Come, sir; since you are eager for the taste of steel, follow me, and say your prayers as you go."

With that we left the inn, amidst a prodigious hubbub, and made our way to the horse-market behind the Hôtel Vendôme. It was not to be expected, albeit the place we had chosen was usually deserted at such an hour, that after the fracas at the "Soleil" our meeting would go unattended. When we faced each other—Canaples and I—there were at least some twenty persons present, who came, despite the rain, to watch what they thought was like to prove a pretty fight. Men of position were they for the most part, gentlemen of the Court with here and there a soldier, and from the manner in which they eyed me methought they favoured me but little.

Our preparations were brief. The absence of seconds disposed of all formalities, the rain made us impatient to be done, and in virtue of it Canaples pompously announced that he would not risk a cold by stripping. With interest did I grimly answer that he need fear no cold when I had done with him. Then casting aside my cloak, I drew, and, professing myself also disposed to retain my doublet, we forthwith engaged.

He was no mean swordsman, this Canaples. Indeed, his reputation was already widespread, and in the first shock of our meeting blades I felt that rumour had been just for once. But I was strangely dispossessed of any doubts touching the outcome; this being due perchance to a vain confidence in my own skill, perchance to the spirit of contemptuous raillery wherewith I had from the outset treated the affair, and which had so taken root in my heart that even when we engaged I still, almost unwittingly, persisted in it.

In my face and attitude there was the reflection of this bantering, flippant mood; it was to be read in the mocking disdain of my glance, in the scornful curl of my lip, and even in the turn of my wrist as I put aside my opponent's passes. All this, Canaples must have noted, and it was not without effect upon his nerves. Moreover, there is in steel a subtle magnetism which is the index of one's antagonist; and from the moment that our blades slithered one against the other I make no doubt but that Canaples grew aware of the confident, almost exultant mood in which I met him, and which told him that I was his master. Add to this the fact that whilst Canaples's nerves were unstrung by passion mine were held in check by a mind as calm and cool as though our swords were baited, and consider with what advantages I took my ground.

He led the attack fiercely and furiously, as if I were a boy whose guard was to be borne down by sheer weight of blows. I contented myself with tapping his blade aside, and when at length, after essaying every trick in his catalogue, he fell back baffled, I laughed a low laugh of derision that drove him pale with fury.

Again he came at me, almost before I was prepared for him, and his point, parried with a downward stroke and narrowly averted, scratched my thigh, but did more damage to my breeches than my skin. in exchange I touched him playfully on the shoulder, and the sting of it drove him back a second time. He was breathing hard by then, and would fain have paused awhile for breath, but I saw no reason to be merciful.

"Now, sir," I cried, saluting him as though our combat were but on the point of starting—"to me! Guard yourself!"

Again our swords clashed, and my blows now fell as swift on his blade as his had done awhile ago on mine. So hard did I press him that he was forced to give way before me. Back I drove him pace by pace, his wrist growing weaker at each parry, each parry growing wider, and the perspiration streaming down his ashen face. Panting he went, in that backward flight before my onslaught, defending himself as best he could, never thinking of a riposte—beaten already. Back, and yet back he went, until he reached the railings and could back no farther, and so broken was his spirit then that a groan escaped him. I answered with a laugh—my mood was lusty and cruel—and thrust at him. Then, eluding his guard, I thrust again, beneath it, and took him fairly in the middle of his doublet.

He staggered, dropped his rapier, and caught at the railings, where for a moment he hung swaying and gasping. Then his head fell forward, his grip relaxed, and swooning he sank down into a heap.

A dozen sprang to his aid, foremost amongst them being St. Auban and Montmédy, whilst I drew back, suddenly realising my own spent condition, to which the heat of the combat had hitherto rendered me insensible. I mastered myself as best I might, and, dissembling my hard breathing, I wiped my blade with a kerchief, an act which looked so calm and callous that it drew from the crowd—for a crowd it had become by then—an angry growl. 'T is thus with the vulgar; they are ever ready to sympathise with the vanquished without ever pausing to ask themselves if his chastisement may not be merited.

In answer to the growl I tossed my head, and sheathing my sword I flung the bloodstained kerchief into their very midst. The audacity of the gesture left them breathless, and they growled no more, but stared.

Then that outrageous fop, Vilmorin, who had been bending over Canaples, started up and coming towards me with a face that was whiter than that of the prostrate man, he proved himself so utterly bereft of wit by terror that for once he had the temerity to usurp the words and actions of a brave man.

"You have murdered him!" he cried in a strident voice, and thrusting his clenched fist within an inch of my face. "Do you hear me, you knave? You have murdered him!"

Now, as may be well conceived, I was in no mood to endure such words from any man, so was but natural that for answer I caught the dainty Vicomte a buffet that knocked him into the arms of the nearest bystander, and brought him to his senses.

"Fool," I snarled at him, "must I make another example before you believe that Gaston de Luynes wears a sword?"

"In the name of Heaven—" he began, putting forth his hands in a beseeching gesture; but what more he said was drowned by the roar of anger that burst from the onlookers, and it was like to have gone ill with me had not St. Auban come to my aid at that most critical juncture.

"Messieurs!" he cried, thrusting himself before me, and raising his hand to crave silence, "hear me. I, a friend of M. de Canaples, tell you that you wrong M. de Luynes. 'T was a fair fight—how the quarrel arose is no concern of yours."

Despite his words they still snarled and growled like the misbegotten curs they were. But St. Auban was famous for the regal supper parties he gave, to which all were eager to be bidden, and amidst that crowd, as I have said, there were a score or so of gentlemen of the Court, who—with scant regard for the right or wrong of the case and every regard to conciliate this giver of suppers—came to range themselves beside and around us, and thus protected me from the murderous designs of that rabble.

Seeing how the gentlemen took my part, and deeming—in their blessed ignorance—that what gentlemen did must be perforce well done, they grew calm in the twinkling of an eye. Thereupon St. Auban, turning to me, counselled me in a whisper to be gone, whilst the tide of opinion flowed in my favour. Intent to act upon this good advice, I took a step towards the little knot that had collected round Canaples, and with natural curiosity inquired into the nature of his hurt.

'T was Montmédy who answered me, scowling as he did so:

"He may die of it, Monsieur. If he does not, his recovery will be at least slow and difficult."

I had been wise had I held my peace and gone; but, like a fool, I must needs give utterance to what was in my mind.

"Ah! At least there will be no duel at St. Germain this evening."

Scarce had the words fallen from my lips when I saw in the faces of Montmédy and St. Auban and half a dozen others the evidence of their rashness.

"So!" cried St. Auban in a voice that shook with rage. "That was your object, eh? That you had fallen low, Master de Luynes, I knew, but I dreamt not that in your fall you had come so low as this."

"You dare?"

"Pardieu! I dare more, Monsieur; I dare tell you—you, Gaston de Luynes, spy and bravo of the Cardinal—that your object shall be defeated. That, as God lives, this duel shall still be fought—by me instead of Canaples."

"And I tell you, sir, that as God lives it shall not," I answered with a vehemence not a whit less than his own. "To you and to what other fools may think to follow in your footsteps, I say this: that not tonight nor tomorrow nor the next day shall that duel be fought. Cowards and poltroons you are, who seek to murder a beardless boy who has injured none of you! But, by my soul! every man who sends a challenge to that boy will I at once seek out and deal with as I have dealt with Eugène de Canaples. Let those who are eager to try another world make the attempt. Adieu, Messieurs!"

And with a flourish of my sodden beaver, I turned and left them before they had recovered from the vehemence of my words.

CHAPTER IV

FAIR RESCUERS

Like the calm of the heavens when pregnant with thunder was the calm of that crowd. And as brief it was; for scarce had I taken a dozen steps when my ears were assailed by a rumble of angry voices and a rush of feet. One glance over my shoulder, one second's hesitation whether I should stay and beard them, then the thought of Andrea de Mancini and of what would befall him did this canaille vent its wrath upon me decided my course and sent me hotfoot down the Rue Monarque. Howling and bellowing that rabble followed in my wake, stumbling over one another in their indecent haste to reach me.

But I was fleet of foot, and behind me there was that that would lend wings to the most deliberate, so that when I turned into the open space before the Hôtel Vendôme I had set a good fifty yards betwixt myself and the foremost of my hunters.

A coach was passing at that moment. I shouted, and the knave who drove glanced at me, then up the Rue Monarque at my pursuers, whereupon, shaking his head, he would have left me to my fate. But I was of another mind. I dashed towards the vehicle, and as it passed me I caught at the window, which luckily was open, and drawing up my legs I hung there despite the shower of mud which the revolving wheels deposited upon me.

From the bowels of the coach I was greeted by a woman's scream; a pale face, and a profusion of fair hair flashed before my eyes.

"Fear not, Madame," I shouted. "I am no assassin, but rather one who stands in imminent peril of assassination, and who craves your protection."

More I would have said, but at that juncture the lash of the coachman's whip curled itself about my shoulders, and stung me vilely.

"Get down, you rascal," he bellowed; "get down or I'll draw rein!"

To obey him would have been madness. The crowd surged behind with hoots and yells, and had I let go I must perforce have fallen into their hands. So, instead of getting down as he inconsiderately counselled, I drew myself farther up by a mighty effort, and thrust half my body into the coach, whereupon the fair lady screamed again, and the whip caressed my legs. But within the coach sat another woman, dark of hair and exquisite of face, who eyed my advent with a disdainful glance. Her proud countenance bore the stamp of courage, and to her it was that I directed my appeal.

"Madame, permit me, I pray, to seek shelter in your carriage, and suffer me to journey a little way with you. Quick, Madame! Your coachman is drawing rein, and I shall of a certainty be murdered under your very nose unless you bid him change his mind. To be murdered in itself is a trifling matter, I avow, but it is not nice to behold, and I would not, for all the world, offend your eyes with the spectacle of it."

I had judged her rightly, and my tone of flippant recklessness won me her sympathy and aid. Quickly thrusting her head through the other window:

"Drive on, Louis," she commanded. "Faster!" Then turning to me, "You may bring your legs into the coach if you choose, sir," she said.

"Your words, Madame, are the sweetest music I have heard for months," I answered drily, as I obeyed her. Then leaning out of the carriage again I waved my hat gallantly to the mob which—now realising the futility of further pursuit—had suddenly come to a halt.

"Au plaisir de vous revoir, Messieurs," I shouted. "Come to me one by one, and I'll keep the devil busy finding lodgings for you."

They answered me with a yell, and I sat down content, and laughed.

"You are not a coward, Monsieur," said the dark lady.

"I have been accounted many unsavoury things, Madame, but my bitterest enemies never dubbed me that."

"Why, then, did you run away?"

"Why? Ma foi! because in the excessive humility of my soul I recognised myself unfit to die."

She bit her lip and her tiny foot beat impatiently upon the floor.

"You are trifling with me, Monsieur. Where do you wish to alight?"

"Pray let that give you no concern; I can assure you that I am in no haste."

"You become impertinent, sir," she cried angrily. "Answer me, where are you going?"

"Where am I going? Oh, ah—to the Palais Royal."

Her eyes opened very wide at that, and wandered over me with a look that was passing eloquent. Indeed, I was a sorry spectacle for any woman's eyes—particularly a pretty one's. Splashed from head to foot with mud, my doublet saturated and my beaver dripping, with the feather hanging limp and broken, whilst there was a rent in my breeches that had been made by Canaples's sword, I take it that I had not the air of a courtier, and that when I said that I went to the Palais Royal she might have justly held me to be the adventurous lover of some kitchen wench. But unto the Palais Royal go others besides courtiers and lovers—spies of the Cardinal, for instance, and in her sudden coldness and the next question that fell from her beauteous lips I read that she had guessed me one of these.

"Why did the mob pursue you, Monsieur?"

There was in her voice and gesture when she asked a question the imperiousness of one accustomed to command replies. This pretty queenliness it was that drove me to answer—as I had done before—in a bantering strain.

"Why did the mob pursue me? Hum! Why does the mob pursue great men? Because it loves their company."

Her matchless eyes flashed an angry glance, and the faint smile on my lips must have tried her temper sorely.

"What did you do to deserve this affection?"

"A mere nothing—I killed a man," I answered coolly. "Or, at least, I left him started on the road to—Paradise."

The little flaxen-haired doll uttered a cry of horror, and covered her face with her small white hands. My inquisitor, however, sat rigid and unaffected. My answer had confirmed her suspicions.

"Why did you kill him?"

"Ma foi!" I replied, encouraging her thoughts, "because he sought to kill me."

"Ah! And why did he seek to kill you?"

"Because I disturbed him at dinner."

"Have a care how you trifle, sir!" she retorted, her eyes kindling again.

"Upon my honour, 't was no more than that. I pulled the cloth from the table whilst he ate. He was a quick-tempered gentleman, and my playfulness offended him. That is all."

Doubt appeared in her eyes, and it may have entered her mind that perchance her judgment had been over-hasty.

"Do you mean, sir, that you provoked a duel?"

"Alas, Madame! It had become necessary. You see, M. de Canaples—"

"Who?" Her voice rang sharp as the crack of a pistol.

"Eh? M. de Canaples."

"Was it he whom you killed?"

From her tone, and the eager, strained expression of her face, it was not difficult to read that some mighty interest of hers was involved in my reply. It needed not the low moan that burst from her companion to tell me so.

"As I have said, Madame, it is possible that he is not dead—nay, even that he will not die. For the rest, since you ask the question, my opponent was, indeed, M. de Canaples—Eugène de Canaples."

Her face went deadly white, and she sank back in her seat as if every nerve in her body had of a sudden been bereft of power, whilst she of the fair hair burst into tears.

A pretty position was this for me!—luckily it endured not. The girl roused herself from her momentary weakness, and, seizing the cord, she tugged it violently. The coach drew up.

"Alight, sir," she hissed—"go! I wish to Heaven that I had left you to the vengeance of the people."

Not so did I; nevertheless, as I alighted: "I am sorry, Madame, that you did not," I answered. "Adieu!"

The coach moved away, and I was left standing at the corner of the Rue St. Honoré and the Rue des Bons Enfants, in the sorriest frame of mind conceivable. The lady in the coach had saved my life, and for that I was more grateful perchance than my life was worth. Out of gratitude sprang a regret for the pain that I had undoubtedly caused her, and the sorrow which it might have been my fate to cast over her life.

Still, regret, albeit an admirable sentiment, was one whose existence was usually brief in my bosom. Dame! Had I been a man of regrets I might have spent the remainder of my days weeping over my past life. But the gods, who had given me a character calculated to lead a man into misfortune, had given me a stout heart wherewith to fight that misfortune, and an armour of recklessness against which remorse, regrets, aye, and conscience itself, rained blows in vain.

And so it befell that presently I laughed myself out of the puerile humour that was besetting me, and, finding myself chilled by inaction in my wet clothes, I set off for the Palais Royal at a pace that was first cousin to a run.

Ten minutes later I stood in the presence of the most feared and hated man in France.

"Cospetto!" cried Mazarin as I entered his cabinet. "Have you swum the Seine in your clothes?"

"No, your Eminence, but I have been serving you in the rain for the past hour."

He smiled that peculiar smile of his that rendered hateful his otherwise not ill-favoured countenance. It was a smile of the lips in which the eyes had no part.

"Yes," he said slowly, "I have heard of your achievements."

"You have heard?" I ejaculated, amazed by the powers which this man wielded.

"Yes, I have heard. You are a brave man, M. de Luynes."

"Pshaw, your Eminence!" I deprecated; "the poor are always brave. They have naught to lose but their life, and that is not so sweet to them that they lay much store by it. Howbeit, Monseigneur, your wishes have been carried out. There will be no duel at St. Germain this evening."

"Will there not? Hum! I am not so confident. You are a brave man, M. de Luynes, but you lack that great auxiliary of valour—discretion. What need to fling into the teeth of those fine gentlemen the reason you had for spitting Canaples, eh? You have provoked a dozen enemies for Andrea where only one existed."

"I will answer for all of them," I retorted boastfully.

"Fine words, M. de Luynes; but to support them how many men will you have to kill? Pah! What if some fine morning there comes one who, despite your vaunted swordsmanship, proves your master? What will become of that fool, my nephew, eh?"

And his uncanny smile again beamed on me. "Andrea is now packing his valise. In an hour he will have left Paris secretly. He goes—but what does it signify where he goes? He is compelled by your indiscretion to withdraw from Court. Had you kept a close tongue in your foolish head—but there! you did not, and so by a thoughtless word you undid all that you had done so well. You may go, M. de Luynes. I have no further need of you—and thank Heaven that you leave the Palais Royal free to go whither your fancy takes you, and not to journey to the Bastille or to Vincennes. I am merciful, M. de Luynes—as merciful as you are brave; more merciful than you are prudent. One word of warning, M. de Luynes: do not let me learn that you are in my nephew's company, if you would not make me regret my clemency and repair the error of it by having you hanged. And now, adieu!"

I stood aghast. Was I indeed dismissed? Albeit naught had been said, I had not doubted, since my interview with him that morning, that did I succeed in saving Andrea my rank in his guards—and thereby a means of livelihood—would be restored to me. And now matters were no better than they had been before. He dismissed me with the assurance that he was merciful. As God lives, it would have been as merciful to have hanged me!

He met my astonished look with an eye that seemed to ask me why I lingered. Then reading mayhap what was passing in my thoughts, he raised a little silver whistle to his lips and blew softly upon it.

"Bernouin," said he to his valet, who entered in answer to the summons, "reconduct M. de Luynes."

I remember drawing down upon my bedraggled person the curious gaze of the numerous clients who thronged the Cardinal's ante-chamber, as I followed Bernouin to the door which opened on to the corridor, and which he held for me. And thus, for the second time within twenty-four hours, did I leave the Palais Royal to wend my way home to the Rue St. Antoine with grim despondency in my heart.

I found Michelot on the point of setting out in search of me, with a note which had been brought to my lodging half an hour ago, and which its bearer had said was urgent. I took the letter, and bidding Michelot prepare me fresh raiment that I might exchange for my wet clothes, I broke the seal and read:

"A thousand thanks, dear friend, for the service you have rendered me and of which his Eminence, my uncle, has informed

35

me. I fear that you have made many enemies for yourself through an action which will likely go unrewarded, and that Paris is therefore as little suited at present to your health as it is to mine. I am setting out for Blois on a mission of exceeding delicacy wherein your advice and guidance would be of infinite value to me. I shall remain at Choisy until tomorrow morning, and should there be no ties to hold you in Paris, and you be minded to bear me company, join me there at the Hôtel du Connétable where I shall lie tonight. Your grateful and devoted

ANDRE."

So! There was one at least who desired my company! I had not thought it. "If there be no ties to hold you in Paris," he wrote. Dame! A change of air would suit me vastly. I was resolved—a fig for the Cardinal's threat to hang me if I were found in his nephew's company!

"My suit of buff, Michelot," I shouted, springing to my feet, "and my leather jerkin."

He gazed at me in surprise.

"Is Monsieur going a journey?"

I answered him that I was, and as I spoke I began to divest myself of the clothes I wore. "Pack my suit of pearl grey in the valise, with what changes of linen I possess; then call Master Coupri that I may settle with him. It may be some time before we return."

In less than half an hour I was ready for the journey, spurred and booted, with my rapier at my side, and in the pocket of my haut-dechausses a purse containing some fifty pistoles—best part of which I had won from Vilmorin at lansquenet some nights before, and which moderate sum represented all the moneys that I possessed.

Our horses were ready, my pistols holstered, and my valise strapped to Michelot's saddle. Despite the desperate outlook of my fortunes, of which I had made him fully cognisant, he insisted upon clinging to me, reminding me that at Rocroi I had saved his life and that he would leave me only when I bade him go.

As four o'clock was striking at Nôtre Dame we crossed the Pont Neuf, and going by the Quai des Augustins and the Rue de la Harpe, we quitted Paris by the St. Michel Gate and took the road to Choisy. The rain had ceased, but the air was keen and cold, and the wind cut like a sword-edge.

CHAPTER V

MAZARIN, THE MATCH-MAKER

Twixt Paris and Choisy there lies but a distance of some two leagues, which, given a fair horse, one may cover with ease in little more than half an hour. So that as the twilight was deepening into night we drew rein before the hostelry of the Connétable, in the only square the little township boasts, and from the landlord I had that obsequious reception which is ever accorded to him who travels with a body-servant.

I found Andrea installed in a fair-sized and comfortable apartment, to the original decoration of which he added not a little by bestowing his boots in the centre of the floor, his hat, sword, and baldrick on the table, his cloak on one chair, and his doublet on another. He himself sat toasting his feet before the blazing logs, which cast a warm, reddish glow upon his sable hair and dainty shirt of cambric.

He sprang up as I entered, and came towards me with a look of pleasure on his handsome, high-bred face, that did me good to see.

"So, you have come, De Luynes," he cried, putting forth his hand. "I did not dare to hope that you would."

"No," I answered. "Truly it was not to be expected that I could be easily lured from Paris just as my fortunes are nearing a high tide, and his Eminence proposing to make me a Marshal of France and create me Duke. As you say, you had scant grounds for hoping that my love for you would suffice to make me renounce all these fine things for the mere sake of accompanying you on your jaunt to Blois."

He laughed, then fell to thanking me for having rid him of Canaples. I cut him short at last, and in answer to his questions told him what had passed 'twixt his Eminence and me that afternoon. Then as the waiter entered to spread our supper, the conversation assumed a less delicate character, until we were again alone with the table and its steaming viands between us.

"You have not told me yet, Andrea, what takes you to Blois," quoth I then.

"You shall learn. Little do you dream how closely interwoven are our morning adventures with this journey of mine. To begin with, I go to Blois to pay my dévoirs to the lady whom his Eminence has selected for my future wife."

"You were then right in describing this as a mission of great delicacy."

"More than you think—I have never seen the lady."

"Never seen her? And you go a-wooing a woman you have never seen?"

"It is so. I have never seen her; but his Eminence has, and 't is he who arranges the affair. Ah, the Cardinal is the greatest matchmaker in France! My cousin Anna Martinozzi is destined for the Prince de Conti, my sisters Olympia and Marianne he also hopes to marry to princes of the blood, whilst I dare wager that he has thoughts of seating either Maria or Hortensia upon the throne of France as the wife of Louis XIV., as soon as his Majesty shall have reached a marriageable age. You may laugh, De Luynes, nevertheless all this may come to pass, for my uncle has great ambitions for his family, and it is even possible that should that poor, wandering youth, Charles II. of England, ever return to the throne of his fathers he may also become my brother-in-law. I am likely to become well connected, De Luynes, so make a friend of me whilst I am humble. So much for Mazarin's nieces. His nephews are too young for alliances just yet, saving myself; and for me his Eminence has chosen one of the greatest heiresses in France—Yvonne St. Albaret de Canaples."

"Whom?" I shouted.

He smiled.

"Curious, is it not? She is the sister of the man whom I quarrelled with this morning, and whom you fought with this afternoon. Now you will understand my uncle's reasons for so strenuously desiring to prevent the duel at St. Germain. It appears that the old Chevalier de Canaples is as eager as the Cardinal to see his daughter wed to me, for his Eminence has promised to create me Duke for a wedding gift. 'T will cost him little, and 't will please these Canaples mightily. Naturally, had Eugène de Canaples and I crossed swords, matters would have been rendered difficult."

"When did you learn all this?" I inquired.

"Today, after the duel, and when it was known what St. Auban and Montmédy had threatened me with. My uncle thought it well that I should withdraw from Paris. He sent for me and told me what I have told you, adding that I had best seize the opportunity, whilst my presence at Court was undesirable, to repair to Blois and get my wooing done. I in part agreed with him. The lady is very rich, and I am told that she is beautiful. I shall see her, and if she pleases me, I'll woo her. If not, I'll return to Paris."

"But her brother will oppose you."

"Her brother? Pooh! If he doesn't die of the sword-thrust you gave him, which I am told is in the region of the lung and passing dangerous, he will at least be abed for a couple of months to come."

"But I, mon cher André? What rôle do you reserve for me, that you have desired me to go with you?"

"The rôle of Mentor if you will. Methought you would prove a merry comrade to help one o'er a tedious journey, and knowing that there was little to hold you to Paris, and probably sound reasons why you should desire to quit it, meseemed that perhaps you would consent to bear me company. Who knows, my knight errant, what adventures may await you and what fortunes? If the heiress displeases me, it may be that she will please you—or mayhap there is another heiress at Blois who will fall enamoured of those fierce moustachios."

I laughed with him at the improbability of such things befalling. I carried in my bosom too large a heart, and one that was the property of every wench I met—for just so long as I chanced to be in her company.

It was no more than in harmony with this habit of mine, that when, next morning in the common-room of the Connétable, I espied Jeanneton, the landlord's daughter, and remarked that she was winsome and shapely, with a complexion that would not have dishonoured a rose-petal, I permitted myself to pinch her dainty cheek. She slapped mine in return, and in this pleasant manner we became acquainted.

"Sweet Jeanneton," quoth I with a laugh, "that was mightily ill-done! I did but pinch your cheek as one may pinch a sweet-smelling bud, so that the perfume of it may cling to one's fingers."

"And I, sir," was the pert rejoinder, "did but slap yours as one may slap a misbehaving urchin's; so that he may learn better manners."

Nevertheless she was pleased with my courtly speech, and perchance also with my moustachios, for a smile took the place of the frown wherewith she had at first confronted me. Now, if I had uttered glib pleasantries in answer to her frowns, how many more did not her smiles wring from me! I discoursed to her in the very courtliest fashion of cows and pullets and such other matters as interesting to her as they were mysterious to me. I questioned her in a breath touching her father's pigs and the swain she loved best in that little township, to all of which she answered me with a charming wit, which would greatly divert you did I but recall her words sufficiently to set them down. In five minutes we had become the best friends in the world, which was attested by the protecting arm that I slipped around her waist, as I asked her whether she loved that village swain of hers better than she loved me, and refused to believe her when she answered that she did.

Outside two men were talking, one calling for a farrier, and when informed that the only one in the village was absent and not likely to return till noon, demanding relays of horses. The other—probably the hostler—answered him that the Connétable was not a post-house and that no horses were to be had there. Then a woman's voice, sweet yet commanding, rose above theirs.

"Very well, Guilbert," it said. "We will await this farrier's return."

"Let me go, Monsieur!" cried Jeanneton. "Some one comes."

Now for myself I cared little who might come, but methought that it was likely to do poor Jeanneton's fair name no benefit, if the arm of Gaston de Luynes were seen about her waist. And so I obeyed her, but not quickly enough; for already a shadow lay athwart the threshold, and in the doorway stood a woman, whose eye took in the situation before we had altered it sufficiently to avert suspicion. To my amazement I beheld the lady of the coach—she who had saved me from the mob in Place Vendôme, and touching whose identity I could have hazarded a shrewd guess.

In her eyes also I saw the light of recognition which swiftly changed to one of scorn. Then they passed from me to the vanishing Jeanneton, and methought that she was about to call her back. She paused, however, and, turning to the lackey who followed at her heels.

"Guilbert," she said, "be good enough to call the landlord, and bid him provide me with an apartment for the time that we may be forced to spend here."

But at this juncture the host himself came hurrying forward with many bows and endless rubbing of hands, which argued untold deference. He regretted that the hostelry of the Connétable, being but a poor inn, seldom honoured as it was at that moment, possessed but one suite of private apartments, and that was now occupied by a most noble gentleman. The lady tapped her foot, and as at that moment her companion (who was none other than the fair-haired doll I had seen with her on the previous day) entered the room, she turned to speak with her, whilst I moved away towards the window.

"Will this gentleman," she inquired, "lend me one of his rooms, think you?"

"Hélas, Mademoiselle, he has but two, a bedroom and an ante-chamber, and he is still abed."

"Oh!" she cried in pretty anger, "this is insufferable! 'T is your fault, Guilbert, you fool. Am I, then, to spend the day here in the common-room?"

"No, no, Mademoiselle," exclaimed the host in his most soothing accents. "Only for an hour, or less, perhaps, until this very noble lord is risen, when assuredly—for he is young and very gallant—he will resign one or both of his rooms to you."

More was said between them, but my attention was suddenly drawn elsewhere. Michelot burst into the room, disaster written on his face.

"Monsieur," he cried, in great alarm, "the Marquis de St. Auban is riding down the street with the Vicomte de Vilmorin and another gentleman."

I rapped out an oath at the news; they had got scent of Andrea's whereabouts, and were after him like sleuth-hounds on a trail.

"Remain here, Michelot," I answered in a low voice. "Tell them that M. de Mancini is not here, that the only occupant of the inn is your master, a gentleman from Normandy, or Picardy, or where you will. See that they do not guess our presence—the landlord fortunately is ignorant of M. de Mancini's name."

There was a clatter of horses' hoofs without, and I was barely in time to escape by the door leading to the staircase, when St. Auban's heavy voice rang out, calling the landlord.

"I am in search of a gentleman named Andrea de Mancini," he said. "I am told that he has journeyed hither, and that he is here at present. Am I rightly informed?"

I determined to remain where I was, and hear that conversation to the end.

"There is a gentleman here," answered the host, "but I am ignorant of his name. I will inquire."

"You may spare yourself the trouble," Michelot interposed. "That is not the gentleman's name. I am his servant."

There was a moment's pause, then came Vilmorin's shrill voice.

"You lie, knave! M. de Mancini is here. You are M. de Luynes's lackey, and where the one is, there shall we find the other."

"M. de Luynes?" came a voice unknown to me. "That is Mancini's sword-blade of a friend, is it not? Well, why does he hide himself? Where is he? Where is your master, rascal?"

"I am here, Messieurs," I answered, throwing wide the door, and appearing, grim and arrogant, upon the threshold.

Mort de ma vie! Had they beheld the Devil, St. Auban and Vilmorin could not have looked less pleased than they did when their eyes lighted upon me, standing there surveying them with a sardonic grin.

St. Auban muttered an oath, Vilmorin stifled a cry, whilst he who had so loudly called to know where I hid myself—a frail little fellow, in the uniform of the gardes du corps—now stood silent and abashed.

The two women, who had withdrawn into a dark and retired corner of the apartment, stood gazing with interest upon this pretty scene.

"Well, gentlemen?" I asked in a tone of persiflage, as I took a step towards them. "Have you naught to say to me, now that I have answered your imperious summons? What! All dumb?"

"Our affair is not with you," said St. Auban, curtly.

"Pardon! Why, then, did you inquire where I was?"

"Messieurs," exclaimed Vilmorin, whose face assumed the pallor usual to it in moments of peril, "meseems we have been misinformed, and that M. de Mancini is not here. Let us seek elsewhere."

"Most excellent advice, gentlemen," I commented,—"seek elsewhere."

"Monsieur," cried the little officer, turning purple, "it occurs to me that you are mocking us."

"Mocking you! Mocking you? Mocking a gentleman who has been tied to so huge a sword as yours. Surely—surely, sir, you do not think—"

"I'll not endure it," he broke in. "You shall answer to me for this."

"Have a care, sir," I cried in alarm as he rushed forward. "Have a care, sir, lest you trip over your sword."

He halted, drew himself up, and, with a magnificent gesture: "I am Armand de Malpertuis, lieutenant of his Majesty's guards," he announced, "and I shall be grateful if you will do me the honour of taking a turn with me, outside."

"I am flattered beyond measure, M. Malappris—"

"Mal-per-tuis," he corrected furiously.

"Malpertuis," I echoed. "I am honoured beyond words, but I do not wish to take a turn."

"Mille diables, sir! Don't you understand? We must fight."

"Must we, indeed? Again I am honoured; but, Monsieur, I don't fight sparrows."

"Gentlemen! Gentlemen!" cried St. Auban, thrusting himself between us. "Malpertuis, have the goodness to wait until one affair is concluded before you create a second one. Now, M. de Luynes, will you tell me whether M. de Mancini is here or not?"

"What if he should be?"

"You will be wise to withdraw—we shall be three to two."

"Three to two! Surely, Marquis, your reckoning is at fault. You cannot count the Vicomte there as one; his knees are knocking together; at best he is but a woman in man's clothes. As for your other friend, unless his height misleads me, he is but a boy. Therefore, Monsieur, you see that the advantage is with us. We are two men opposed to a man, a woman, and a child, so that—"

"In Heaven's name, sir," cried St. Auban, again interposing himself betwixt me and the bellicose Malpertuis, "will you cease this foolishness? A word with you in private, M. de Luynes."

I permitted him to take me by the sleeve, and lead me aside, wondering the while what curb it was that he was setting upon his temper, and what wily motives he might have for adopting so conciliatory a tone.

With many generations to come, the name of César de St. Auban must perforce be familiar as that of one of the greatest roysterers and most courtly libertines of the early days of Louis XIV., as well as that of a rabid anti-cardinalist and frondeur, and one of the earliest of that new cabal of nobility known as the petits-maîtres, whose leader the Prince de Condé was destined to become a few years later. He was a man of about my own age, that is to say, between thirty-two and thirty-three, and of my own frame, tall, spare, and active. On his florid, débonnair countenance was stamped his character of bon-viveur. In dress he was courtly in the extreme. His doublet and haut-de-chausses were of wine-coloured velvet, richly laced, and he still affected the hanging sleeves of a fast-disappearing fashion. Valuable lace filled the tops of his black boots, a valuable jewel glistened here and there upon his person, and one must needs have pronounced him a fop but for the strength and resoluteness of his bearing, and the long rapier that hung from his gold-embroidered baldrick. Such in brief is a portrait of the man who now confronted me, his fine blue eyes fixed upon my face, wherein methinks he read but little, search though he might.

"M. de Luynes," he murmured at last, "you appear to find entertainment in making enemies, and you do it wantonly."

"Have you brought me aside to instruct me in the art of making friends?"

"Possibly, M. de Luynes; and without intending an offence, permit me to remark that you need them."

"Mayhap. But I do not seek them."

"I have it in my heart to wish that you did; for I, M. de Luynes, seek to make a friend of you. Nay, do not smile in that unbelieving fashion. I have long esteemed you for those very qualities of dauntlessness and defiance which have brought you so rich a crop of hatred. If you doubt

46

my words, perhaps you will recall my attitude towards you in the horse-market yesterday, and let that speak. Without wishing to remind you of a service done, I may yet mention that I stood betwixt you and the mob that sought to avenge my friend Canaples. He was my friend; you stood there, as indeed you have always stood, in the attitude of a foe. You wounded Canaples, maltreated Vilmorin, defied me; and yet but for my intervention, mille diables sir, you had been torn to pieces."

"All this I grant is very true, Monsieur," I made reply, with deep suspicion in my soul. "Yet, pardon me, if I confess that to me it proves no more than that you acted as a generous enemy. Pardon my bluntness also— but what profit do you look to make from gaining my friendship?"

"You are frank, Monsieur," he said, colouring slightly, "I will be none the less so. I am a frondeur, an anti-cardinalist. In a word, I am a gentleman and a Frenchman. An interloping foreigner, miserly, mean-souled, and Jesuitical, springs up, wins himself into the graces of a foolish, impetuous, wilful queen, and climbs the ladder which she holds for him to the highest position in France. I allude to Mazarin; this Cardinal who is not a priest; this minister of France who is not a Frenchman; this belittler of nobles who is not a gentleman."

"Mort Dieu, Monsieur—"

"One moment, M. de Luynes. This adventurer, not content with the millions which his avaricious talons have dragged from the people for his own benefit, seeks, by means of illustrious alliances, to enrich a pack of beggarly nieces and nephews that he has rescued from the squalor of their Sicilian homes to bring hither. His nieces, the Mancinis and Martinozzis, he is marrying to Dukes and Princes. 'T is not nice to witness, but 't is the affair of the men who wed them. In seeking, however, to marry his nephew Andrea to one of the greatest heiresses in France, he goes too far. Yvonne de Canaples is for some noble countryman of her own—there are many suitors to her hand—and for no nephew of Giulio Mazarini. Her brother Eugène, himself, thinks thus, and therein, M. de Luynes, you have the real motive of the quarrel which he provoked with Andrea, and which, had you not interfered, could have had but one ending."

"Why do you tell me all this, Monsieur?" I inquired coldly, betraying none of the amazement his last words gave birth to.

"So that you may know the true position of affairs, and, knowing it, see the course which the name you bear must bid you follow. Because Canaples failed am I here today. I had not counted upon meeting you, but since I have met you, I have set the truth before you, confident that you will now withdraw from an affair to which no real interest can bind you, leaving matters to pursue their course."

He eyed me, methought, almost anxiously from under his brows, as he awaited my reply. It was briefer than he looked for.

"You have wasted time, Monsieur."

"How? You persist?"

"Yes. I persist. Yet for the Cardinal I care nothing. Mazarin has dismissed me from his service unjustly and unpaid. He has forbidden me his nephew's company. In fact, did he know of my presence here with M. de Mancini, he would probably carry out his threat to hang me."

"Ciel!" cried St. Auban, "you are mad, if that be so. France is divided into two parties, cardinalists and anti-cardinalists. You, sir, without belonging to either, stand alone, an enemy to both. Your attitude is preposterous!"

"Nay, sir, not alone. There is Andrea de Mancini. The boy is my only friend in a world of enemies. I am growing fond of him, Monsieur, and I will stand by him, while my arm can wield a sword, in all that may advance his fortunes and his happiness. That, Monsieur, is my last word."

"Do not forget, M. de Luynes," he said—his suaveness all departed of a sudden, and his tone full of menace and acidity—"do not forget that when a wall may not be scaled it may be broken through."

"Aye, Monsieur, but many of those who break through stand in danger of being crushed by the falling stones," I answered, entering into the spirit of his allegory.

"There are many ways of striking," he said.

"And many ways of being struck," I retorted with a sneer.

Our words grew sinister, our eyes waxed fiery, and more might have followed had not the door leading to the staircase opened at that moment to admit Andrea himself. He came, elegant in dress and figure, with a smile upon his handsome young face, whose noble features gave the lie to St. Auban's assertion that he had been drawn from a squalid Sicilian home. Such faces are not bred in squalor.

In utter ignorance of the cabal against him, he greeted St. Auban—who was well known to him—with a graceful bow, and also Vilmorin, who stood in the doorway with Malpertuis, and who at the sight of Mancini grew visibly ill at ease. In coming to Choisy, the Vicomte had clearly expected to do no more than second St. Auban in the duel which he thought to see forced upon Andrea. He now realised that if a fight there was, he might, by my presence, be forced into it. Malpertuis looked fierce and tugged at his moustachios, whilst his companions returned Andrea's salutation—St. Auban gravely, and Vilmorin hesitatingly.

"Ha, Gaston," said the boy, advancing towards me, "our host tells me that two ladies who have been shipwrecked here wish to do me the honour of occupying my apartments for an hour or so. Ha, there they are," he added, as the two girls came suddenly forward. Then bowing—"Mesdames, I am enchanted to set the poor room at your disposal for as long as it may please you to honour it."

As the ladies—of whose presence St. Auban had been unaware—appeared before us, I shot a glance at the Marquis, and, from the start he gave upon beholding them, I saw that things were as I had suspected.

Before they could reply to Andrea, St. Auban suddenly advanced:

"Mesdemoiselles," quoth he, "forgive me if in this miserable light I did not earlier discover your presence and offer you my services. I do so now, with the hope that you will honour me by making use of them."

"Merci, M. de St. Auban," replied the dark-haired one—whom I guessed to be none other than Yvonne de Canaples herself—"but, since this gentleman so gallantly cedes his apartments to us, all our needs are satisfied. It would be churlish to refuse that which is so graciously proffered."

Her tone was cold in the extreme, as also was the inclination of her head wherewith she favoured the Marquis. In arrant contrast were the pretty words of thanks she addressed to Andrea, who stood by, blushing like a girl, and a damnable scowl did this contrast draw from St. Auban, a scowl that lasted until, escorted by the landlord, the two ladies had withdrawn.

There was an awkward pause when they were gone, and methought from the look on St. Auban's face that he was about to provoke a fight after all. Not so, however, for, after staring at us like a clown whilst one might tell a dozen, he turned and strode to the door, calling for his horse and those of his companions.

"Au révoir, M. de Luynes," he said significantly as he got into the saddle.

"Au révoir, M. de Luynes," said also Malpertuis, coming close up to me. "We shall meet again, believe me."

"Pray God that we may not, if you would die in your bed," I answered mockingly. "Adieu!"

CHAPTER VI

OF HOW ANDREA BECAME LOVE-SICK

With what fictions I could call to mind I put off Andrea's questions touching the peculiar fashion of St. Auban's leave-taking. Tell him the truth and expose to him the situation whereof he was himself the unconscious centre I dared not, lest his high-spirited impetuosity should cause him to take into his own hands the reins of the affair, and thus drive himself into irreparable disaster.

Andrea himself showed scant concern, however, and was luckily content with my hurriedly invented explanations; his thoughts had suddenly found occupation in another and a gentler theme than the ill-humour of men, and presently his tongue betrayed them when he drew the conversation to the ladies to whom he had resigned his apartments.

"Pardieu! Gaston," he burst out, "she is a lovely maid—saw you ever a bonnier?"

"Indeed she is very beautiful," I answered, laughing to myself at the thought of how little he dreamt that it was of Yvonne St. Albaret de Canaples that he spoke, and not minded for the while to enlighten him.

"If she be as kind and gentle as she is beautiful, Gaston, well—Uncle Giulio's plans are likely to suffer shipwreck. I shall not leave Choisy until I have spoken to her; in fact, I shall not leave until she leaves."

"Nevertheless, we shall still be able to set out, as we had projected, after dining, for in an hour, or two at most, they will proceed on their journey."

He was silent for some moments, then:

"To the devil with the Cardinal's plans!" quoth he, banging his fist on the table. "I shall not go to Blois."

"Pooh! Why not?"

"Why not?" He halted for a moment, then in a meandering tone— "You have read perchance in story-books," he said, "of love being born from the first meeting of two pairs of eyes, as a spark is born of flint and steel, and you may have laughed at the conceit, as I have laughed at it. But laugh no more, Gaston; for I who stand before you am one who has experienced this thing which poets tell of, and which hitherto I have held in ridicule. I will not go to Blois because—because—enfin, because I intend to go where she goes."

"Then, mon cher, you will go to Blois. You will go to Blois, if not as a dutiful nephew, resigned to obey his reverend uncle's wishes, at least because fate forces you to follow a pair of eyes that have—hum, what was it you said they did?"

"Do you say that she is going to Blois? How do you know?"

"Eh? How do I know? Oh, I heard her servant speaking with the hostler."

"So much the better, then; for thus if his Eminence gets news of my whereabouts, the news will not awaken his ever-ready suspicions. Ciel! How beautiful she is! Noted you her eyes, her skin, and what hair, mon Dieu! Like threads of gold!"

"Like threads of gold?" I echoed. "You are dreaming, boy. Oh, St. Gris! I understand; you are speaking of the fair-haired chit that was with her."

He eyed me in amazement.

"'T is you whose thoughts are wandering to that lanky, nose-in-the-air Madame who accompanied her."

I began a laugh that I broke off suddenly as I realised that it was not Yvonne after all who had imprisoned his wits. The Cardinal's plans were, indeed, likely to miscarry if he persisted thus.

"But 't was the nose-in-the-air Madame, as you call her, with whom you spoke!"

"Aye, but it was the golden-haired lady that held my gaze. Pshaw! Who would mention them in a breath?"

"Who, indeed?" said I, but with a different meaning.

Thereafter, seeing him listless, I suggested a turn in the village to stretch our limbs before dining. But he would have none of it, and when I pressed the point with sound reasoning touching the benefits which health may cull from exercise, he grew petulant as a wayward child. She might descend whilst he was absent. Indeed, she might require some slight service that lay, perchance, in his power to render her. What an opportunity would he not lose were he abroad? She might even depart before we returned; and than that no greater calamity could just then befall him. No, he would not stir a foot from the inn. A fig for exercise! to the devil with health! who sought an appetite? Not he. He wished for no appetite—could contrive no base and vulgar appetite for food, whilst his soul, he swore, was being consumed by the overwhelming, all-effacing appetite to behold her.

Such meandering fools are most of us at nineteen, when the heart is young—a flawless mirror ready to hold the image of the first fair maid that looks into it through our eyes, and as ready—Heaven knows!—to relinquish it when the substance is withdrawn.

But I, who was not nineteen, and the mirror of whose heart—to pursue my metaphor—was dulled, warped, and cracked with much illusage, grew sick of the boy's enthusiasm and the monotony of a conversation which I could divert into no other channel from that upon which it had been started by a little slip of a girl with hair of gold and sapphire eyes—I use Andrea's words. And so I rose, and bidding him take root in the tavern, if so it pleased his fancy, I left him there.

Wrapped in my cloak, for the air was raw and damp, I strode aimlessly along, revolving in my mind what had befallen at the Connétable that morning, and speculating upon the issue that this quaint affair might have. In matters of love, or rather, of matrimony—which is not quite the same thing—opposition is common enough. But the opposers are usually members of either of the interested families. Now the families—that is to say, the heads of the families—being agreed and even anxious to bring about the union of Yvonne de Canaples and Andrea de Mancini, it was something new to have a cabal of persons who, from motives of principle—as St. Auban had it—should oppose the alliance so relentlessly as to even resort to violence if no other means occurred to them. It seemed vastly probable that Andrea would be disposed of by a knife in the back, and more than probable that a like fate would be reserved for me, since I had constituted myself his guardian angel. For my own part, however, I had a pronounced distaste to ending my days in so unostentatious a fashion. I had also a notion that I should prove an exceedingly difficult person to assassinate, and that those who sought to slip a knife into me would find my hide peculiarly tough, and my hand peculiarly ready to return the compliment.

So deeply did I sink into ponderings of this character that it was not until two hours afterwards that I again found myself drawing near the Connétable.

I reached the inn to find by the door a coach, and by that coach Andrea; he stood bareheaded, despite the cold, conversing, with all outward semblances of profound respect, with those within it.

So engrossed was he and so ecstatic, that my approach was unheeded, and when presently I noted that the coach was Mademoiselle de Canaples's, I ceased to wonder at the boy's unconsciousness of what took place around him.

Clearly the farrier had been found at last, and the horse shod afresh during my absence. Loath to interrupt so pretty a scene, I waited, aloof, until these adieux should be concluded, and whilst I waited there came to me from the carriage a sweet, musical voice that was not Yvonne's.

"May we not learn at least, Monsieur, the name of the gentleman to whose courtesy we are indebted for having spent the past two hours without discomfort?"

"My name, Mademoiselle, is Andrea de Mancini, that of the humblest of your servants, and one to whom your thanks are a more than lavish payment for the trivial service he may have been fortunate enough to render you."

Dame! What glibness doth a tongue acquire at Court!

"M. Andrea de Mancini?" came Yvonne's voice in answer. "Surely a relative of the Lord Cardinal?"

"His nephew, Mademoiselle."

"Ah! My father, sir, is a great admirer of your uncle."

From the half-caressing tone, as much as from the very words she uttered, I inferred that she was in ignorance of the compact into which his Eminence had entered with her father—a bargain whereof she was herself a part.

"I am rejoiced, indeed, Mademoiselle," replied Andrea with a bow, as though the compliment had been paid to him. "Am I indiscreet in asking the name of Monsieur your father?"

"Indiscreet! Nay, Monsieur. You have a right to learn the name of those who are under an obligation to you. My father is the Chevalier de Canaples, of whom it is possible that you may have heard. I am Yvonne de Canaples, of whom it is unlikely that you should have heard, and this is my sister Geneviève, whom a like obscurity envelops."

The boy's lips moved, but no sound came from them, whilst his cheeks went white and red by turns. His courtliness of a moment ago had vanished, and he stood sheepish and gauche as a clown. At length he so far mastered himself as to bow and make a sign to the coachman, who thereupon gathered up his reins.

"You are going presumably to Blois?" he stammered with a nervous laugh, as if the journey were a humorous proceeding.

"Yes, Monsieur," answered Geneviève, "we are going home."

"Why, then, it is possible that we shall meet again. I, too, am travelling in that direction. A bientôt, Mesdemoiselles!"

The whip cracked, the coach began to move, and the creaking of its wheels drowned, so far as I was concerned, the female voices that answered his farewell. The coachman roused his horses into an amble; the amble became a trot, and the vehicle vanished round a corner. Some few idlers stopped to gaze stupidly after it, but not half so stupidly as did my poor Andrea, standing bareheaded where the coach had left him.

I drew near, and laid my hand on his shoulder; at the touch he started like one awakened suddenly, and looked up.

"Ah—you are returned, Gaston."

"To find that you have made a discovery, and are overwhelmed by your error."

"My error?"

"Yes—that of falling in love with the wrong one. Hélas, it is but one of those ironical jests wherewith Fate amuses herself at every step of our lives. Had you fallen in love with Yvonne—and it passes my understanding why you did not—everything would have gone smoothly with your wooing. Unfortunately, you have a preference for fair hair—"

"Have done," he interrupted peevishly. "What does it signify? To the devil with Mazarin's plans!"

"So you said this morning."

"Yes, when I did not even dream her name was Canaples."

"Nevertheless, she is the wrong Canaples."

"For my uncle—but, mille diables! sir, 't is I who am to wed, and I shall wed as my heart bids me."

"Hum! And Mazarin?"

"Faugh!" he answered, with an expressive shrug.

"Well, since you are resolved, let us dine."

"I have no appetite."

"Let us dine notwithstanding. Eat you must if you would live; and unless you live—think of it!—you'll never reach Blois."

"Gaston, you are laughing at me! I do not wish to eat."

I surveyed him gravely, with my arms akimbo.

"Can love so expand the heart of man that it fills even his stomach? Well, well, if you will not eat, at least have the grace to bear me company at table. Come, Andrea," and I took his arm, "let us ascend to that chamber which she has but just quitted. Who can tell but that we shall find there some token of her recent presence? If nothing more, at least the air will be pervaded by the perfume she affected, and since you scorn the humble food of man, you can dine on that."

He smiled despite himself as I drew him towards the staircase.

"Scoffer!" quoth he. "Your callous soul knows naught of love."

"Whereas you have had three hours' experience. Pardieu! You shall instruct me in the gentle art."

Alas, for those perfumes upon which I had proposed that he should feast himself. If any the beautiful Geneviève had left behind her, they had been smothered in the vulgar yet appetising odour of the steaming ragoût that occupied the table.

I prevailed at length upon the love-lorn boy to take some food, but I could lead him to talk of naught save Geneviève de Canaples. Presently he took to chiding me for the deliberateness wherewith I ate, and betrayed thereby his impatience to be in the saddle and after her. I argued that whilst she saw him not she might think of him. But the argument, though sound, availed me little, and in the end I was forced—for all that I am a man accustomed to please myself—to hurriedly end my repast, and pronounce myself ready to start.

As Andrea had with him some store of baggage—since his sojourn at Blois was likely to be of some duration—he travelled in a coach. Into this coach, then, we climbed—he and I. His valet, Silvio, occupied the seat beside the coachman, whilst my stalwart Michelot rode behind leading my horse by the bridle. In this fashion we set out, and ere long the silence of my thoughtful companion, the monotonous rumbling of the vehicle, and, most important of all factors, the good dinner that I had consumed, bred in me a torpor that soon became a sleep.

From a dream that, bound hand and foot, I was being dragged by St. Auban and Malpertuis before the Cardinal, I awakened with a start to find that we were clattering already through the streets of Etrechy; so that whilst I had slept we had covered some six leagues. Twilight had already set in, and Andrea lay back idly in the carriage, holding a book which it was growing too dark to read, and between the leaves of which he had slipped his forefinger to mark the place where he had paused.

His eyes met mine as I looked round, and he smiled. "I should not have thought, Gaston," he said, "that a man with so seared a conscience could have slept thus soundly."

"I have not slept soundly," I grumbled, recalling my dream.

"Pardieu! you have slept long, at least."

"Out of self-protection; so that I might not hear the name of Geneviève de Canaples. 'T is a sweet name, but you render it monotonous."

He laughed good-humouredly.

"Have you never loved, Gaston?"

"Often."

"Ah—but I mean did you never conceive a great passion?"

"Hundreds, boy."

"But never such a one as mine!"

"Assuredly not; for the world has never seen its fellow. Be good enough to pull the cord, you Cupid incarnate. I wish to alight."

"You wish to alight! Why?"

"Because I am sick of love. I am going to ride awhile with Michelot whilst you dream of her coral lips, her sapphire eyes, and what other gems constitute her wondrous personality."

Two minutes later I was in the saddle riding with Michelot in the wake of the carriage. As I have already sought to indicate in these pages, Michelot was as much my friend as my servant. It was therefore no more than natural that I should communicate to him my fears touching what might come of the machinations of St. Auban, Vilmorin, and even, perchance, of that little firebrand, Malpertuis.

Night fell while we talked, and at last the lights of Étampes, where we proposed to lie, peeped at us from a distance, and food and warmth.

It was eight o'clock when we reached the town, and a few moments later we rattled into the courtyard of the Hôtel de l'Épée.

Andrea was out of temper to learn that Mesdemoiselles de Canaples had reached the place two hours earlier, taken fresh horses, and proceeded on their journey, intending to reach Monnerville that night. He was even mad enough to propose that we should follow their example, but my sober arguments prevailed, and at Étampes we stayed till morning.

Andrea withdrew early. But I, having chanced upon a certain M. de la Vrillière, a courtier of Vilmorin's stamp, with whom I had some slight acquaintance, and his purse being heavier than his wits, I spent a passing profitable evening in his company. This pretty gentleman hailed my advent with a delight that amazed me, and suggested that we should throw a main together to kill time. The dice were found, and so clumsily did he use them that in half an hour, playing for beggarly crowns, he had lost twenty pistoles. Next he lost his temper, and with an oath pitched the cubes into the fire, swearing that they were toys for children and that I must grant him his révanche with cards. The cards were furnished us, and with a fortune that varied little we played lansquenet until long past midnight. The fire died out in the grate, and the air grew chill, until at last, with a violent sneeze, La Vrillière protested that he would play no more.

Cursing himself for the unluckiest being alive, the fool bade me goodnight, and left me seventy pistoles richer than when I had met him.

CHAPTER VII

THE CHÂTEAU DE CANAPLES

Despite the strenuous efforts which Andrea compelled us to put forth, we did not again come up with Mesdemoiselles de Canaples, who in truth must have travelled with greater speed than ladies are wont to.

This circumstance bred much discomfort in Andrea's bosom; for in it he read that his Geneviève thought not of him as he of her, else, knowing that he followed the same road, she would have retarded their progress so that he might overtake them. Thus argued he when on the following night, which was that of Friday, we lay at Orleans. But when towards noon on Saturday our journey ended with our arrival at Blois, he went so far as to conclude that she had hastened on expressly to avoid him. Now, from what I had seen of Mademoiselle Yvonne, methought I might hazard a guess that she it was who commanded in these—and haply, too, in other—matters, and that the manner of their journey had been such as was best to her wishes.

With such an argument did I strive to appease Andrea's doubts; but all in vain—which is indeed no matter for astonishment, for to reason with a man in love is to reason with one who knows no reason.

After a brief halt at the Lys de France—at which hostelry I hired myself a room—we set out for the Château de Canaples, which is situated on the left bank of the Loire, at a distance of about half a league from Blois in the direction of Tours.

We cut a brave enough figure as we rode down the Rue Vieille attended by our servants, and many a rustic Blaisois stopped to gape at us, to nudge his companion, and point us out, whispering the word "Paris."

I had donned my grey velvet doublet—deeming the occasion worthy of it—whilst Andrea wore a handsome suit of black, with gold lace, which for elegance it would have been difficult to surpass. An air of pensiveness added interest to his handsome face and courtly figure, and methought that Geneviève must be hard to please if she fell not a victim to his wooing.

We proceeded along the road bordering the Loire, a road of rare beauty at any other season of the year, but now bare of foliage, grey, bleak, and sullen as the clouds overhead, and as cold to the eye as was the sharp wind to the flesh. As we rode I fell to thinking of what my reception at the Château de Canaples was likely to be, and almost to regret that I had permitted Andrea to persuade me to accompany him. Long ago I had known the Chevalier de Canaples, and for all the disparity in our ages—for he counted twice my years—we had been friends and comrades. That, however, was ten years ago, in the old days when I owned something more than the name of Luynes. Today I appeared before him as a ruined adventurer, a soldier of fortune, a ruffler, a duellist who had almost slain his son in a brawl, whose details might be known to him, but not its origin. Seeing me in the company of Andrea de Mancini he might—who could say?—even deem me one of those parasites who cling to young men of fortune so that they may live at their expense. That the daughter would have formed such a conceit of me I was assured; it but remained to see with what countenance the father would greet me.

From such speculations I was at length aroused by our arrival at the gates of the Canaples park. Seeing them wide open, we rode between the two massive columns of granite (each surmounted by a couchant lion holding the escutcheon of the Canaples) and proceeded at an ambling pace up the avenue. Through the naked trees the château became discernible—a brave old castle that once had been the stronghold of a feudal race long dead. Grey it was, and attuned, that day, to the rest of the grey landscape. But at its base the ivy grew thick and green, and here and there long streaks of it crept up almost to the battlements, whilst in one place it had gone higher yet and clothed one of the quaint old turrets. A moat there had once been, but this was now filled up and arranged into little mounds that became flower-beds in summer.

Resigning our horses to the keeping of our servants, we followed the grave maître d'hôtel who had received us. He led us across the spacious hall, which had all the appearance of an armoury, and up the regal staircase of polished oak on to a landing wide and lofty. Here, turning to the left, he opened a door and desired us to give ourselves the trouble of awaiting the Chevalier. We entered a handsome room, hung in costly Dutch tapestry, and richly furnished, yet with a sobriety of colour almost puritanical. The long windows overlooked a broad terrace, enclosed in a grey stone balustrade, from which some half-dozen steps led to a garden below. Beyond that ran the swift waters of the Loire, and beyond that again, in the distance, we beheld the famous Château de Chambord, built in the days of the first Francis.

I had but remarked these details when the door again opened, to admit a short, slender man in whose black hair and beard the hand of time had scattered but little of that white dust that marks its passage. His face was pale, thin, and wrinkled, and his grey eyes had a nervous, restless look that dwelt not long on anything. He was dressed in black, with simple elegance, and his deep collar and ruffles were of the finest point.

"Welcome to Canaples, M. de Mancini!" he exclaimed, as he hurried forward, with a smile so winning that his countenance appeared transfigured by it. "Welcome most cordially! We had not hoped that you would arrive so soon, but fortunately my daughters, to whom you appear to have been of service at Choisy, warned me that you were journeying hither. Your apartments, therefore, are prepared for you, and we hope that you will honour Canaples by long remaining its guest."

Andrea thanked him becomingly.

"In truth," he added, "my departure from Paris was somewhat sudden, but I have a letter here from Monseigneur my uncle, which explains the matter."

"No explanation is needed, my dear Andrea," replied the old nobleman, abandoning the formalities that had marked his welcoming speech. "How left you my Lord Cardinal?" he asked, as he took the letter.

"In excellent health, but somewhat harassed, I fear, by the affairs of State."

"Ah, yes, yes. But stay. You are not alone." And Canaples's grey eyes shot an almost furtive glance of inquiry in my direction. A second glance followed the first and the Chevalier's brows were knit. Then he came a step nearer, scanning my face.

"Surely, surely, Monsieur," he exclaimed before Andrea had time to answer him. "Were you not at Rocroi?"

"Your memory flatters me, Monsieur," I replied with a laugh. "I was indeed at Rocroi—captain in the regiment of chévaux-légers whereof you were Mestre de Champ."

"His name," said Andrea, "is Gaston de Luynes, my very dear friend, counsellor, and, I might almost say, protector."

"Pardieu, yes! Gaston de Luynes!" he ejaculated, seizing my hand in an affectionate grip. "But how have you fared since Rocroi was fought? For a soldier of such promise, one might have predicted great things in ten years."

"Hélas, Monsieur! I was dismissed the service after Senlac."

"Dismissed the service!"

"Pah!" I laughed, not without bitterness, 't is a long story and an ugly one, divided 'twixt the dice-box, the bottle, and the scabbard. Ten years ago I was a promising young captain, ardent and ambitious; today I am a broken ruffler, unrecognised by my family—a man without hope, without ambition, almost without honour."

I know not what it was that impelled me to speak thus. Haply the wish that since he must soon learn to what depths Gaston de Luynes had sunk, he should at least learn it from my own lips at the outset.

He shuddered at my concluding words, and had not Andrea at that moment put his arm affectionately upon my shoulder, and declared me the bravest fellow and truest friend in all the world, it is possible that the Chevalier de Canaples would have sought an excuse to be rid of me. Such men as he seek not the acquaintance of such men as I.

To please Andrea was, however, of chief importance in his plans, and to that motive I owe it that he pressed me to remain a guest at the château. I declined the honour with the best grace I could command, determined that whilst Andrea remained at Canaples I would lodge at the Lys de France in Blois, independent and free to come or go as my fancy bade me. His invitation that I should at least dine at Canaples I accepted; but with the condition that he should repeat his invitation after he had heard something that I wished to tell him. He assented with a puzzled look, and when presently Andrea repaired to his apartments, and we were alone, I began.

"You have doubtlessly received news, Monsieur, of a certain affair in which your son had recently the misfortune to be dangerously wounded?"

We were standing by the great marble fireplace, and Canaples was resting one of his feet upon the huge brass andirons. He made a gesture of impatience as I spoke.

"My son, sir, is a fool! A good-for-nothing fool! Oh, I have heard of this affair, a vulgar tavern brawl, the fifth in which his name has been involved and besmirched. I had news this morning by a courier dispatched me by my friend St. Simon, who imagines that I am deeply concerned in that young profligate. I learn that he is out of danger, and that in a month or so, he will be about again and ready to disgrace the name of Canaples afresh. But there, sir; I crave your pardon for the interruption."

64

I bowed, and when in answer to my questions he told me that he was in ignorance of the details of the affair of which I spoke, I set about laying those details before him. Beginning with the original provocation in the Palais Royal and ending with the fight in the horse-market, I related the whole story to him, but in an impersonal manner, and keeping my own name out of my narrative. When I had done, Canaples muttered an oath of the days of the fourth Henry.

"Ventre St. Gris! Does the dog carry his audacity so far as to dare come betwixt me and my wishes, and to strive against them? He sought to kill Mancini, eh? Would to Heaven he had died by the hand of this fellow who shielded the lad!"

"Monsieur!" I cried, aghast at so unnatural an expression.

"Pah!" he cried harshly. "He is my son in name alone, filial he never was."

"Nevertheless, Monsieur, he is still your son, your heir."

"My heir? And what, pray, does he inherit? A title—a barren, landless title! By his shameful conduct he alienated the affection of his uncle, and his uncle has disinherited him in favour of Yvonne. 'T is she who will be mistress of this château with its acres of land reaching from here to Blois, and three times as far on the other side. My brother, sir, was the rich Canaples, the owner of all this, and by his testament I am his heir during my lifetime, the estates going to Yvonne at my death. So that you see I have naught to leave; but if I had, not a dénier should go to my worthless son!"

He spread his thin hands before the blaze, and for a moment there was silence. Then I proceeded to tell him of the cabal which had been formed against Mancini, and of the part played by St. Auban. At the mention of that name he started as if I had stung him.

"What!" he thundered. "Is that ruffian also in the affair? Sangdieu! His motives are not far to seek. He is a suitor—an unfavoured suitor— for the hand of Yvonne, that seemingly still hopes. But you have not told me, Monsieur, the name of this man who has stood betwixt Andrea and his assassins."

"Can you not guess, Monsieur?" quoth I, looking him squarely in the face. "Did you not hear Andrea call me, even now, his protector."

"You? And with what motive, pray?"

"At first, as I have told you, because the Cardinal gave me no choice in the matter touching your son. Since then my motive has lain in my friendship for the boy. He has been kind and affectionate to one who has known little kindness or affection in life. I seek to repay him by advancing his interests and his happiness. That, Monsieur, is why I am here today—to shield him from St. Auban and his fellows should they appear again, as I believe they will."

The old man stood up and eyed me for a moment as steadily as his vacillating glance would permit him, then he held out his hand.

"I trust, Monsieur," he said, "that you will do me the honour to dine with us, and that whilst you are at Blois we shall see you at Canaples as often as it may please you to cross its threshold."

I took his hand, but without enthusiasm, for I understood that his words sprang from no warmth of heart for me, but merely from the fact that he beheld in me a likely ally to his designs of raising his daughter to the rank of Duchess.

Eugène de Canaples may have been a good-for-nothing knave; still, methought his character scarce justified the callous indifference manifested by this selfish, weak-minded old man towards his own son.

There was a knock at the door, and a lackey—the same Guilbert whom I had seen at Choisy in Mademoiselle's company—appeared with the announcement that the Chevalier was served.

CHAPTER VIII

THE FORESHADOW OF DISASTER

In the spacious dining salon of the Château de Canaples I found the two daughters of my host awaiting us—those same two ladies of the coach in Place Vendôme and of the hostelry at Choisy, the dark and stately icicle, Yvonne, and the fair, playful doll, Geneviève.

I bowed my best bow as the Chevalier presented me, and from the corner of my eye, with inward malice, I watched them as I did so. Geneviève curtsied with a puzzled air and a sidelong glance at her sister. Yvonne accorded me the faintest, the coldest, inclination of her head, whilst her cheeks assumed a colour that was unwonted.

"We have met before, I think, Monsieur," she said disdainfully.

"True, Mademoiselle—once," I answered, thinking only of the coach.

"Twice, Monsieur," she corrected, whereupon I recalled how she had surprised me with my arm about the waist of the inn-keeper's daughter, and had Heaven given me shame I might have blushed. But if sweet Yvonne thought to bring Gaston de Luynes to task for profiting by the good things which God's providence sent his way, she was led by vanity into a prodigious error.

"Twice, indeed, Mademoiselle. But the service which you rendered me upon the first occasion was so present to my mind just now that it eclipsed the memory of our second meeting. I have ever since desired, Mademoiselle, that an opportunity might be mine wherein to thank you for the preservation of my life. I do so now, and at your service do I lay that life which you preserved, and which is therefore as much yours as mine."

Strive as I might I could not rid my tone of an ironical inflection. I was goaded to it by her attitude, by the scornful turn of her lip and the disdainful glance of her grey eyes—she had her father's eyes, saving that her gaze was as steadfast as his was furtive.

"What is this?" quoth Canaples. "You owe your life to my daughter? Pray tell me of it."

"With all my heart," I made haste to answer before Mademoiselle could speak. "A week ago, I disagreed upon a question of great delicacy with a certain gentleman who shall be nameless. The obvious result attended our disagreement, and we fought 'neath the eyes of a vast company of spectators. Right was on my side, and the gentleman hurt himself upon my sword. Well, sir, the crowd snarled at me as though it were my fault that this had so befallen, and I flouted the crowd in answer. They were a hundred opposed to one, and so confident did this circumstance render them of their superiority, that for once those whelps displayed sufficient valour to attack me. I fled, and as a coach chanced to come that way, I clutched at the window and hung there. Within the coach there were two ladies, and one of them, taking compassion upon me, invited me to enter and thus rescued me. That lady, sir," I ended with a bow, "was Mademoiselle your daughter."

In his eyes I read it that he had guessed the name of my nameless gentleman.

The ladies were struck dumb by my apparent effrontery. Yvonne at last recovered sufficiently to ask if my presence at the château arose from my being attached to M. de Mancini. Now, "attached" is an unpleasant word. A courtier is attached to the King; a soldier to the army; there is humiliation in neither of these. But to a private gentleman, a man may be only attached as his secretary, his valet, or, possibly, as his bravo. Therein lay the sting of her carefully chosen word.

68

"I am M. de Mancini's friend," I answered with simple dignity.

For all reply she raised her eyebrows in token of surprise; Canaples looked askance; I bit my lip, and an awkward silence followed, which, luckily, was quickly ended by the appearance of Andrea.

The ladies received him graciously, and a faint blush might, to searching eyes, have been perceived upon Geneviève's cheek.

There came a delicate exchange of compliments, after which we got to table, and for my part I did ample justice to the viands.

I sat beside Geneviève, and vis-à-vis with Andrea, who occupied the place of the honoured guest, at the host's right hand, with Yvonne beside him. Me it concerned little where I sat, since the repast was all that I could look for; not so the others. Andrea scowled at me because I was nearer to Geneviève than he, and Yvonne frowned at me for other reasons. By Geneviève I was utterly disregarded, and my endeavours to converse were sorely unsuccessful—for one may not converse alone.

I clearly saw that Yvonne only awaited an opportunity to unmask me, and denounce me to her father as the man who had sought his son's life.

This opportunity, however, came not until the moment of my departure from the château, that evening. I was crossing the hail with the Chevalier de Canaples, and we had stopped for a moment to admire a piece of old chain armour of the days of the Crusaders. Andrea and Geneviève had preceded us, and passed out through the open doorway, whilst Yvonne lingered upon the threshold looking back.

"I trust, M. de Luynes," said Canaples, as we moved towards her, "that you will remember my invitation, and that whilst you remain at Biois we shall see you here as often as you may be pleased to come; indeed, I trust that you will be a daily visitor."

Before I could utter a reply—"Father," exclaimed Mademoiselle, coming forward, "do you know to whom you are offering the hospitality of Canaples?"

"Why that question, child? To M. de Luynes, M. de Mancini's friend."

"And the would-be murderer of Eugène," she added fiercely.

Canaples started.

"Surely such affairs are not for women to meddle with," he cried. "Moreover, M. de Luynes has already given me all details of the affair."

Her eyes grew very wide at that.

"He has told you? Yet you invite him hither?" she exclaimed.

"M. de Luynes has naught wherewith to reproach himself, nor have I. Those details which he has given me I may not impart to you; suffice it, however, that I am satisfied that his conduct could not have been other than it was, whereas that of my son reflects but little credit upon his name."

She stamped her foot, and her eyes, blazing with anger, passed from one to the other of us.

"And you—you believe this man's story?"

"Yvonne!"

"Possibly," I interposed, coolly, "Mademoiselle may have received some false account of it that justifies her evident unbelief in what I may have told you."

It is not easy to give a lie unless you can prove it a lie. I made her realise this, and she bit her lip in vexation. Dame! What a pretty viper I thought her at that moment!

"Let me add, Yvonne," said her father, "that M. de Luynes and I are old comrades in arms." Then turning to me—"My daughter, sir, is but a child, and therefore hasty to pass judgment upon matters beyond her understanding. Forget this foolish outburst, and remember only my assurance of an ever cordial welcome."

"With all my heart," I answered, after a moment's deliberation, during which I had argued that for once I must stifle pride if I would serve Andrea.

"Ough!" was all Mademoiselle's comment as she turned her back upon me. Nevertheless, I bowed and flourished my beaver to her retreating figure.

Clearly Mademoiselle entertained for me exactly that degree of fondness which a pious hermit feels for the devil, and if I might draw conclusions from what evidences I had had of the strength of her character and the weakness of her father's, our sojourn at Blois promised to afford me little delectation. In fact, I foresaw many difficulties that might lead to disaster should our Paris friends appear upon the scene—a contingency this that seemed over-imminent.

It was not my wont, howbeit, to brood over the evils that the future might hold, and to this I owe it that I slept soundly that night in my room at the Lys de France.

It was a pleasant enough chamber on the first floor, overlooking the street, and having an alcove attached to it which served for Michelot.

Next day I visited the Château de Canaples early in the afternoon. The weather was milder, and the glow of the sun heralded at last the near approach of spring and brightened wondrously a landscape that had yesterday worn so forbidding a look.

This change it must have been that drew the ladies, and Andrea with them, to walk in the park, where I came upon them as I rode up. Their laughter rippled merrily and they appeared upon the best of terms until they espied me. My advent was like a cloud that foretells a storm, and drove Mesdemoiselles away, when they had accorded me a greeting that contained scant graciousness.

All unruffled by this act, from which I gathered that Yvonne the strong had tutored Geneviève the frail concerning me, I consigned my horse to a groom of the château, and linked arms with Andrea.

"Well, boy," quoth I, "what progress?"

He smiled radiantly.

"My hopes are all surpassed. It exceeds belief that so poor a thing as I should find favour in her eyes—what eyes, Gaston!" He broke off with a sigh of rapture.

"Peste, you have lost no time. And so, already you know that you find favour, eh! How know you that?"

"How? Need a man be told such things? There is an inexpressible—
"

"My good Andrea, seek not to express it, therefore," I interrupted hastily. "Let it suffice that the inexpressible exists, and makes you happy. His Eminence will doubtless share your joy! Have you written to him?"

The mirth faded from the lad's face at the words, as the blossom fades 'neath the blighting touch of frost. What he said was so undutiful from a nephew touching his uncle—particularly when that uncle is a prelate—that I refrain from penning it.

We were joined just then by the Chevalier, and together we strolled round to the rose-garden—now, alas! naught but black and naked bushes—and down to the edge of the Loire, yellow and swollen by the recent rains.

"How lovely must be this place in summer," I mused, looking across the water towards Chambord. "And, Dame," I cried, suddenly changing my meditations, "what an ideal fencing ground is this even turf!"

"The swordsman's instinct," laughed Canaples.

And with that our talk shifted to swords, swordsmen, and sword-play, until I suggested to Andrea that he should resume his practice, whereupon the Chevalier offered to set a room at our disposal.

"Nay, if you will pardon me, Monsieur, 't is not a room we want," I answered. "A room is well enough at the outset, but it is the common error of fencing-masters to continue their tutoring on a wooden floor. It results from this that when the neophyte handles a real sword, and defends his life upon the turf, the ground has a new feeling; its elasticity or even its slipperiness discomposes him, and sets him at a disadvantage."

He agreed with me, whilst Andrea expressed a wish to try the turf. Foils were brought, and we whiled away best part of an half-hour. In the end, the Chevalier, who had watched my play intently, offered to try a bout with me. And so amazed was he with the result, that he had not done talking of it when I left Canaples a few hours later—a homage this that earned me some more than ordinarily unfriendly glances from

Yvonne. No doubt since the accomplishment was mine it became in her eyes characteristic of a bully and a ruffler.

During the week that followed I visited the château with regularity, and with equal regularity did Andrea receive his fencing lessons. The object of his presence at Canaples, however, was being frustrated more and more each day, so far as the Cardinal and the Chevalier were concerned.

He raved to me of Geneviève, the one perfect woman in all the world and brought into it by a kind Providence for his own particular delectation. In truth, love is like a rabid dog—whom it bites it renders mad; so open grew his wooing, and so ardent, that one evening I thought well to take him aside and caution him.

"My dear Andrea," said I, "if you will love Geneviève, you will, and there's an end of it. But if you would not have the Chevalier pack you back to Paris and the anger of my Lord Cardinal, be circumspect, and at least when M. de Canaples is by divide your homage equally betwixt the two. 'T were well if you dissembled even a slight preference for Yvonne—she will not be misled by it, seeing how unmistakable at all other seasons must be your wooing of Geneviève."

He was forced to avow the wisdom of my counsel, and to be guided by it.

Nevertheless, I rode back to my hostelry in no pleasant frame of mind. It was more than likely that a short shrift and a length of hemp would be the acknowledgment I should anon receive from Mazarin for my participation in the miscarriage of his desires.

I felt that disaster was on the wing. Call it a premonition; call it what you will. I know but this; that as I rode into the courtyard of the Lys de France, at dusk, the first man my eyes alighted on was the Marquis César de St. Auban, and, in conversation with him, six of the most arrant-looking ruffians that ever came out of Paris.

CHAPTER IX

OF HOW A WHIP PROVED A BETTER ARGUMENT THAN A TONGUE

"I crave Monsieur's pardon, but there is a gentleman below who desires to speak with you immediately."

"How does this gentleman call himself, M. l'Hote?"

"M. le Marquis de St. Auban," answered the landlord, still standing in the doorway.

It wanted an hour or so to noon on the day following that of St. Auban's arrival at Blois, and I was on the point of setting out for the château on an errand of warning.

It occurred to me to refuse to see the Marquis, but remembering betimes that from your enemy's speech you may sometimes learn where to look for his next attack, I thought better of it and bade my host admit him.

I strode over to the fire, and stirring the burning logs, I put my back to the blaze, and waited.

Steps sounded on the stairs; there was the shuffling of the landlord's slippered feet and the firm tread of my visitor, accompanied by the jingle of spurs and the clank of his scabbard as it struck the balustrade. Then my door was again opened, and St. Auban, as superbly dressed as ever, was admitted.

We bowed formally, as men bow who are about to cross swords, and whilst I waited for him to speak, I noted that his face was pale and bore the impress of suppressed anger.

"So, M. de Luynes, again we meet."

"By your seeking, M. le Marquis."

"You are not polite."

"You are not opportune."

He smiled dangerously.

"I learn, Monsieur, that you are a daily visitor at the Château de Canaples."

"Well, sir, what of it?"

"This. I have been to Canaples this morning and, knowing that you will learn anon, from that old dotard, what passed between us, I prefer that you shall hear it first from me."

I bowed to conceal a smile.

"Thanks to you, M. de Luynes, I was ordered from the house. I—César de St. Auban—have been ordered from the house of a provincial upstart! Thanks to the calumnies which you poured into his ears."

"Calumnies! Was that the word?"

"I choose the word that suits me best," he answered, and the rage that was in him at the affront he had suffered at the hands of the Chevalier de Canaples was fast rising to the surface. "I warned you at Choisy of what would befall. Your opposition and your alliance with M. de Mancini are futile. You think to have gained a victory by winning over to your side an old fool who will sacrifice his honour to see his daughter a duchess, but I tell you, sir—"

"That you hope to see her a marchioness," I put in calmly. "You see, M. de St. Auban, I have learned something since I came to Blois."

He grew livid with passion.

"You shall learn more ere you quit it, you meddler! You shall be taught to keep that long nose of yours out of matters that concern you not."

I laughed.

"Loud threats!" I answered jeeringly.

"Never fear," he cried, "there is more to follow. To your cost shall you learn it. By God, sir! do you think that I am to suffer a Sicilian adventurer and a broken tavern ruffler to interfere with my designs?"

Still I kept my temper.

"So!" I said in a bantering tone. "You confess that you have designs. Good! But what says the lady, eh? I am told that she is not yet outrageously enamoured of you, for all your beauty!"

Beside himself with passion, his hand sought his sword. But the gesture was spasmodic.

"Knave!" he snarled.

"Knave to me? Have a care, St. Auban, or I'll find you a shroud for a wedding garment."

"Knave!" he repeated with a snarl. "What price are you paid by that boy?"

"Pardieu, St. Auban! You shall answer to me for this."

"Answer for it? To you!" And he laughed harshly. "You are mad, my master. When did a St. Auban cross swords with a man of your stamp?"

"M. le Marquis," I said, with a calmness that came of a stupendous effort, "at Choisy you sought my friendship with high-sounding talk of principles that opposed you to the proposed alliance, twixt the houses of Mancini and Canaples. Since then I have learned that your motives were purely personal. From my discovery I hold you to be a liar."

"Monsieur!"

"I have not yet done. You refuse to cross swords with me on the pretext that you do not fight men of my stamp. I am no saint, sir, I confess. But my sins cannot wash out my name—the name of a family accounted as good as that of St. Auban, and one from which a Constable of France has sprung, whereas yours has never yet bred aught but profligates and debauchees. You are little better than I am, Marquis; indeed, you do many things that I would not do, that I have never done. For instance, whilst refusing to cross blades with me, who am a soldier and a man of the sword, you seek to pick a fight with a beardless boy who hardly knows the use of a rapier, and who—wittingly at least—has done you no wrong. Now, my master, you may call me profligate, ruffler, gamester, duellist— what you will; but there are two viler things you cannot dub me, and which, methinks, I have proven you to be—liar and craven."

And as I spoke the burning words, I stood close up to him and tapped his breast as if to drive the epithets into his very heart.

Rage he felt, indeed, and his distorted countenance was a sight fearful to behold.

"Now, my master," I added, setting my arms akimbo and laughing brutally in his face, "will you fight?"

For a moment he wavered, and surely meseemed that I had drawn him. Then:

"No," he cried passionately. "I will not do dishonour to my sword." And turning he made for the door, leaving me baffled.

"Go, sir," I shouted, "but fame shall stalk fast behind you. Liar and craven will I dub you throughout the whole of France."

He stopped 'neath the lintel, and faced me again.

"Fool," he sneered. "You'll need dispatch to spread my fame so far. By this time tomorrow you'll be arrested. In three days you will be in the Bastille, and there shall you lie until you rot to carrion."

"Loud threats again!" I laughed, hoping by the taunt to learn more.

"Loud perchance, but not empty. Learn that the Cardinal has knowledge of your association with Mancini, and means to separate you. An officer of the guards is on his way to Blois. He is at Meung by now. He bears a warrant for your arrest and delivery to the governor of the Bastille. Thereafter, none may say what will betide." And with a coarse burst of laughter he left me, banging the door as he passed out.

For a moment I stood there stricken by his parting words. He had sought to wound me, and in this he had succeeded. But at what cost to himself? In his blind rage, the fool had shown me that which he should have zealously concealed, and what to him was but a stinging threat was to me a timely warning. I saw the necessity for immediate action. Two things must I do; kill St. Auban first, then fly the Cardinal's warrant as best I could. I cast about me for means to carry out the first of these intentions. My eye fell upon my riding-whip, lying on a chair close to my hand, and the sight of it brought me the idea I sought. Seizing it, I bounded out of the room and down the stairs, three steps at a stride.

Along the corridor I sped and into the common-room, which at the moment was tolerably full. As I entered by one door, the Marquis was within three paces of the other, leading to the courtyard.

My whip in the air, I sprang after him; and he, hearing the rush of my onslaught, turned, then uttered a cry of pain as I brought the lash caressingly about his shoulders.

"Now, master craven," I shouted, "will that change your mind?"

With an almost inarticulate cry, he sought to draw there and then, but those about flung themselves upon us, and held us apart—I, passive and unresisting; the Marquis, bellowing, struggling, and foaming at the mouth.

"To meet you now would be to murder you, Marquis," I said coolly. "Send your friends to me to appoint the time."

"Soit!" he cried, his eyes blazing with a hate unspeakable. "At eight tomorrow morning I shall await you on the green behind the castle of Blois."

"At eight o'clock I shall be there," I answered. "And now, gentlemen, if you will unhand me, I will return to my apartments."

They let me go, but with many a growl and angry look, for in their eyes I was no more than a coarse aggressor, whilst their sympathy was all for St. Auban.

CHAPTER X

THE CONSCIENCE OF MALPERTUIS

And so back to my room I went, my task accomplished, and so pleased was I with what had passed that as I drew on my boots—preparing to set out to Canaples—I laughed softly to myself.

St. Auban I would dispose of in the morning. As for the other members of the cabal, I deemed neither Vilmorin nor Malpertuis sufficiently formidable to inspire uneasiness. St. Auban gone, they too would vanish. There remained then Eugène de Canaples. Him, however, methought no great evil was to be feared from. In Paris he might be as loud-voiced as he pleased, but in his father's château—from what I had learned—'t was unlikely he would so much as show himself. Moreover, he was wounded, and before he had sufficiently recovered to offer interference it was more than probable that Andrea would have married one or the other of Mesdemoiselles de Canaples—though I had a shrewd suspicion that it would be the wrong one, and there again I feared trouble.

As I stood up, booted and ready to descend, there came a gentle tap at my door, and, in answer to my "Enter," there stood before me a very dainty and foppish figure. I stared hard at the effeminate face and the long fair locks of my visitor, thinking that I had become the dupe of my eyes.

"M. de Vilmorin!" I murmured in astonishment, as he came forward, having closed the door. "You here?"

In answer, he bowed and greeted me with cold ceremoniousness.

"I have been in Blois since yesterday, Monsieur."

"In truth I might have guessed it, Vicomte. Your visit flatters me, for, of course, I take it, you are come to pay me your respects," I said ironically. "A glass of wine, Vicomte?"

"A thousand thanks, Monsieur—no," he answered coldly in his mincing tones. "It is concerning your affair with M. le Marquis de St. Auban that I am come." And drawing forth a dainty kerchief, which filled the room with the scent of ambregris, he tapped his lips with it affectedly.

"Do you come as friend or—in some other capacity?"

"I come as mediator."

"Mediator!" I echoed, and my brow grew dark. "Sdeath! Has St. Auban's courage lasted just so long as the sting of my whip?"

He raised his eyebrows after a supercilious fashion that made me thirst to strike the chair from under him.

"You misapprehend me; M. de St. Auban has no desire to avert the duel. On the contrary, he will not rest until the affront you have put upon him be washed out—"

"It will be, I'll answer for it."

"Your answer, sir, is characteristic of a fanfarron. He who promises most does not always fulfil most."

I stared at him in amazement.

"Shall I promise you something, Vicomte? Mortdieu! If you seek to pick a quarrel with me—"

"God forbid!" he ejaculated, turning colour. And his suddenly awakened apprehensions swept aside the affectation that hitherto had marked his speech and manner.

"Then, Monsieur, be brief and state the sum of this mediation."

"It is this, Monsieur. In the heat of the moment, M. le Marquis gave you, in the hearing of half a score of people, an assignation for tomorrow morning. News of the affair will spread rapidly through Blois, and it is likely there will be no lack of spectators on the green to witness the

80

encounter. Therefore, as my friend thinks this will be as unpalatable to you as it is to him, he has sent me to suggest a fresh rendezvous."

"Pooh, sir," I answered lightly. "I care not, for myself, who comes. I am accustomed to a crowd. Still, since M. de St. Auban finds it discomposing, let us arrange otherwise."

"There is yet another point. M. de St. Auban spoke to you, I believe, of an officer who is coming hither charged with your arrest. It is probable that he may reach Blois before morning, so that the Marquis thinks that to make certain you might consent to meet him tonight."

"Ma foi. St. Auban is indeed in earnest then! Convey to him my expressions of admiration at this suddenly awakened courage. Be good enough, Vicomte, to name the rendezvous."

"Do you know the chapel of St. Sulpice des Reaux?"

"What! Beyond the Loire?"

"Precisely, Monsieur. About a league from Chambord by the river side."

"I can find the place."

"Will you meet us there at nine o'clock tonight?"

I looked askance at him.

"But why cross the river? This side affords many likely spots!"

"Very true, Monsieur. But the Marquis has business at Chambord this evening, after which there will be no reason—indeed, it will inconvenience him exceedingly—to return to Blois."

"What!" I cried, more and more astonished. "St. Auban is leaving Blois?"

"This evening, sir."

"But, voyons, Vicomte, why make an assignation in such a place and at night, when at any hour of the day I can meet the Marquis on this side, without suffering the inconvenience of crossing the river?"

"There will be a bright moon, well up by nine o'clock. Moreover, remember that you cannot, as you say, meet St. Auban on this side at any time he may appoint, since tonight or tomorrow the officer who is in search of you will arrive."

I pondered for a moment. Then:

"M. le Vicomte," I said, "in this matter of ground 't is I who have the first voice."

"How so?"

"Because the Marquis is the affronted one."

"Therefore he has a right to choose."

"A right, yes. But that is not enough. The necessity to fight is on his side. His honour is hurt, not mine; I have whipped him; I am content. Now let him come to me."

"Assuredly you will not be so ungenerous."

"I do not care about journeying to Reaux to afford him satisfaction."

"Does Monsieur fear anything?"

"Vicomte, you go too far!" I cried, my pride gaining the mastery. "Since it is asked of me,—I will go."

"M. le Marquis will be grateful to you."

"A fig for his gratitude," I answered, whereupon the Vicomte shrugged his narrow shoulders, and, his errand done, took his leave of me.

When he was gone I called Michelot, to tell him of the journey I must go that night, so that he might hold himself in readiness.

"Why—if Monsieur will pardon me," quoth he, "do you go to meet the Marquis de St. Auban at St. Sulpice des Reaux by night?"

"Precisely what I asked Vilmorin. The Marquis desires it, and—what will you?—since I am going to kill the man, I can scarce do less than kill him on a spot of his own choosing."

Michelot screwed up his face and scratched at his grey beard with his huge hand.

"Does no suspicion of foul play cross your mind, Monsieur?" he inquired timidly.

"Shame on you, Michelot," I returned with some heat. "You do not yet understand the ways of gentlemen. Think you that M. de St. Auban would stoop to such a deed as that? He would be shamed for ever! Pooh, I would as soon suspect my Lord Cardinal of stealing the chalices from Nôtre Dame. Go, see to my horse. I am riding to Canaples."

As I rode out towards the château I fell to thinking, and my thoughts turning to Vilmorin, I marvelled at the part he was playing in this little comedy of a cabal against Andrea de Mancini. His tastes and instincts were of the boudoir, the ante-chamber, and the table. He wore a sword because it was so ordained by fashion, and because the hilt was convenient for the display of a jewel or two. Certainly 't was not for utility that it hung beside him, and no man had ever seen it drawn. Nature had made him the most pitiable coward begotten. Why then should he involve himself in an affair which promised bloodshed, and which must be attended by many a risk for him? There was in all this some mystery that I could not fathom.

From the course into which they had slipped, my thoughts were diverted, when I was within half a mile of the château, by the sight of a horseman stationed, motionless, among the trees that bordered the road. It occurred to me that men take not such a position without purpose— usually an evil one. I slackened speed somewhat and rode on, watching him sharply. As I came up, he walked his horse forward to meet me, and I beheld a man in the uniform of the gardes du corps, in whom presently I recognised the little sparrow Malpertuis, with whom I had exchanged witticisms at Choisy. He was the one man wanting to complete the trinity that had come upon us at the inn of the Connétable.

It flashed across my mind that he might be the officer charged with my arrest, and that he had arrived sooner than had been expected. If so, it was likely to go ill with him, for I was not minded to be taken until St. Auban's soul sped hellwards.

He hailed me as I advanced, and indeed rode forward to meet me.

"You are come at last, M. de Luynes," was his greeting. "I have waited for you this hour past."

"How knew you I should ride this way?"

"I learnt that you would visit Canaples before noon. Be good enough to quit the road, and pass under those trees with me. I have something to say to you, but it were not well that we should be seen together."

"For the sake of your character or mine, M. Malappris?"

"Malpertuis!" he snapped.

"Malpertuis," I corrected. "You were saying that we should not be seen together."

"St. Auban might hear of it."

"Ah! And therefore?"

"You shall learn." We were now under the trees, which albeit leafless yet screened us partly from the road. He drew rein, and I followed his example.

"M. de Luynes," he began, "I am or was a member of the cabal formed against Mazarin's aims in the matter of the marriage of Mademoiselle de Canaples to his nephew. I joined hands with St. Auban, lured by his protestations that it is not meet that such an heiress as Yvonne de Canaples should be forced to marry a foreigner of no birth and less distinction, whilst France holds so many noble suitors to her hand. This motive, by which I know that even Eugène de Canaples was actuated, was, St. Auban gave me to understand, his only one for embarking upon this business, as it was also Vilmorin's. Now, M. de Luynes, I have today discovered that I had been duped by St. Auban and his dupe, Vilmorin. St. Auban lied to me; another motive brings him into the affair. He seeks himself, by any means that may present themselves, to marry Yvonne—and her estates; whilst the girl, I am told, loathes him beyond expression. Vilmorin again is actuated by no less a purpose. And so, what think you these two knaves—this master knave and his dupe—have determined? To carry off Mademoiselle by force!"

"Sangdieu!" I burst out, and would have added more, but his gesture silenced me, and he continued:

"Vilmorin believes that St. Auban is helping him in this, whereas St. Auban is but fooling him with ambiguous speeches until they have the lady safe. Then might will assert itself, and St. Auban need but show his fangs to drive the sneaking coward away from the prize he fondly dreams is to be his."

"When do these gentlemen propose to carry out their plan? Have they determined that?" I inquired breathlessly.

"Aye, they have. They hope to accomplish it this very day. Mademoiselle de Canaples has received a letter wherein she is asked to meet her anonymous writer in the coppice yonder, at the Angelus this evening, if she would learn news of great importance to her touching a conspiracy against her father."

"Faugh!" I sneered. "'T is too poor a bait to lure her with."

"Say you so? Believe me that unless she be dissuaded she will comply with the invitation, so cunningly was the letter couched. A closed carriage will be waiting at this very spot. Into this St. Auban, Vilmorin, and their bravos will thrust the girl, then away through Blois and beyond it, for a mile or so, in the direction of Meung, thereby misleading any chance pursuers. There they will quit the coach and take a boat that is to be in waiting for them and which will bear them back with the stream to Chambord. Thereafter, God pity the poor lady if they get thus far without mishap."

"Mort de ma vie!" I cried, slapping my thigh, "I understand!" And to myself I thought of the assignation at St. Sulpice des Reaux, and the reason for this, as also St. Auban's resolution to so suddenly quit Blois, grew of a sudden clear to me. Also did I recall the riddle touching Vilmorin's conduct which a few moments ago I had puzzled over, and of which methought that I now held the solution.

"What do you understand?" asked Malpertuis.

"Something that was told me this morning," I made answer, then spoke of gratitude, wherein he cut me short.

"I ask no thanks," he said curtly. "You owe me none. What I have done is not for love of you or Mancini—for I love neither of you. It is done because noblesse m'oblige. I told St. Auban that I would have no part in this outrage. But that is not enough; I owe it to my honour to attempt the frustration of so dastardly a plan. You, M. de Luynes, appear to be the most likely person to encompass this, in the interests of your friend Mancini; I leave the matter, therefore, in your hands. Goodday!"

And with this abrupt leave-taking, the little fellow doffed his hat to me, and wheeling his horse he set spurs in its flanks, and was gone before a word of mine could have stayed him.

CHAPTER XI

OF A WOMAN'S OBSTINACY

"M. de Luynes is a wizard," quoth Andrea, laughing, in answer to something that had been said.

It was afternoon. We had dined, and the bright sunshine and spring-like mildness of the weather had lured us out upon the terrace. Yvonne and Geneviève occupied the stone seat. Andrea had perched himself upon the granite balustrade, and facing them he sat, swinging his shapely legs to and fro as he chatted merrily, whilst on either side of him stood the Chevalier de Canaples and I.

"If M. de Luynes be as great a wizard in other things as with the sword, then, pardieu, he is a fearful magician," said Canaples.

I bowed, yet not so low but that I detected a sneer on Yvonne's lips.

"So, pretty lady," said I to myself, "we shall see if presently your lip will curl when I show you something of my wizard's art."

And presently my chance came. M. de Canaples found reason to leave us, and no sooner was he gone than Geneviève remembered that she had that day discovered a budding leaf upon one of the rose bushes in the garden below. Andrea naturally caused an argument by asserting that she was the victim of her fancy, as it was by far too early in the year. By that means these two found the plea they sought for quitting us, since neither could rest until the other was convinced.

So down they went into that rose garden which methought was like to prove their fool's paradise, and Yvonne and I were left alone. Then she also rose, but as she was on the point of quitting me:

"Mademoiselle," I ventured, "will you honour me by remaining for a moment? There is something that I would say to you."

With raised eyebrows she gave me a glance mingled with that superciliousness which she was for ever bestowing upon me, and which, from the monotony of it alone, grew irksome.

"What can you have to say to me, M. de Luynes?"

"Will you not be seated? I shall not long detain you, nevertheless—"

"If I stand, perchance you will be more brief. I am waiting, Monsieur."

I shrugged my shoulders rudely. Why, indeed, be courteous where so little courtesy was met with?

"A little while ago, Mademoiselle, when M. de Mancini dubbed me a wizard you were good enough to sneer. Now, a sneer, Mademoiselle, implies unbelief, and I would convince you that you were wrong to disbelieve."

"If you have no other motive for detaining me, suffer me to depart," she interrupted with some warmth. "Whether you be a wizard or not is of no moment to me."

"And yet I dare swear that you will be of a different mind within five minutes. A wizard is one who discloses things unknown to his fellow-men. I am about to convince you that I can do this, and by convincing you I am about to serve you."

"I seek neither conviction nor service at your hands," she answered.

"Your courtesy dumfounds me, Mademoiselle!"

"No less than does your insolence dumfound me," she retorted, with crimson cheeks. "Do you forget, sir, that I know you for what you are—a gamester, a libertine, a duellist, the murderer of my brother?"

"That your brother lives, Mademoiselle, is, methinks, sufficient proof that I have not murdered him."

"You willed his death if you did not encompass it; so 't is all one. Do you not understand that it is because my father receives you here, thanks to M. de Mancini, your friend—a friendship easily understood from the advantages you must derive from it—that I consent to endure your presence and the insult of your glance? Is it not enough that I should do this, and have you not wit enough to discern it, without adding to my shame by your insolent call upon my courtesy?"

Her words cut me as no words that I ever heard, and, more than her words, her tone of loathing and disgust unspeakable. For half that speech I should have killed a man—indeed, I had killed men for less than half. And yet, for all the passion that raged in my soul, I preserved upon my countenance a smiling mask. That smile exhausted her patience and increased her loathing, for with a contemptuous exclamation she turned away.

"Tarry but a moment, Mademoiselle," I cried, with a sudden note of command. "Or, if you will go, go then; but take with you my assurance that before nightfall you will weep bitterly for it."

My words arrested her. The mystery of them awakened her curiosity.

"You speak in riddles, Monsieur."

"Like a true wizard, Mademoiselle. You received a letter this morning in a handwriting unknown, and bearing no signature."

She wheeled round and faced me again with a little gasp of astonishment.

"How know you that? Ah! I understand; you wrote it!"

"What shrewdness, Mademoiselle!" I laughed, ironically. "Come; think again. What need have I to bid you meet me in the coppice yonder? May I not speak freely with you here?"

"You know the purport of that letter?"

"I do, Mademoiselle, and I know more. I know that this hinted conspiracy against your father is a trumped-up lie to lure you to the coppice."

"And for what purpose, pray?"

"An evil one,—your abduction. Shall I tell you who penned that note, and who awaits you? The Marquis César de St. Auban."

She shuddered as I pronounced the name, then, looking me straight between the eyes—"How come you to know these things?" she inquired.

"What does it signify, since I know them?"

"This, Monsieur, that unless I learn how, I can attach no credit to your preposterous story."

"Not credit it!" I cried. "Let me assure you that I have spoken the truth; let me swear it. Go to the coppice at the appointed time, and things will fall out as I have predicted."

"Again, Monsieur, how know you this?" she persisted, as women will.

"I may not tell you."

We stood close together, and her clear grey eyes met mine, her lip curling in disdain.

"You may not tell me? You need not. I can guess." And she tossed her shapely head and laughed. "Seek some likelier story, Monsieur. Had you not spoken of it, 't is likely I should have left the letter unheeded. But your disinterested warning has determined me to go to this rendezvous. Shall I tell you what I have guessed? That this conspiracy against my father, the details of which you would not have me learn, is some evil of your own devising. Ah! You change colour!" she cried, pointing to my face. Then with a laugh of disdain she left me before I had sufficiently recovered from my amazement to bid her stay.

"Ciel!" I cried, as I watched the tall, lissom figure vanish through the portals of the château. "Did ever God create so crass and obstinate a thing as woman?"

It occurred to me to tell Andrea, and bid him warn her. But then she would guess that I had prompted him. Naught remained but to lay the matter before the Chevalier de Canaples. Already I had informed him of my fracas with St. Auban, and of the duel that was to be fought that night, and he, in his turn, had given me the details of his stormy interview with the Marquis, which had culminated in St. Auban's dismissal from Canaples. I had not hitherto deemed it necessary to alarm him with the news imparted to me by Malpertuis, imagining that did I inform Mademoiselle that would suffice.

Now, however, as I have said, no other course was left me but to tell him of it. Accordingly, I went within and inquired of Guilbert, whom I met in the hall, where I might find the Chevalier. He answered me that M. de Canaples was not in the château. It was believed that he had gone with M. Louis, the intendant of the estates, to visit the vineyards at Montcroix.

The news made me choke with impatience. Already it was close upon five o'clock, and in another hour the sun would set and the Angelus would toll the knell of Mademoiselle's preposterous suspicions, unless in the meantime I had speech with Canaples, and led him to employ a father's authority to keep his daughter indoors.

Fuming at the contretemps I called for my horse and set out at a brisk trot for Montcroix. But my ride was fruitless. The vineyard peasants had not seen the Chevalier for over a week.

Now, 'twixt Montcroix and the château there lies a good league, and to make matters worse, as I galloped furiously back to Canaples, an evil chance led me to mistake the way and pursue a track that brought me out on the very banks of the river, with a strong belt of trees screening the château from sight, and defying me to repair my error by going straight ahead.

I was forced to retrace my steps, and before I had regained the point where I had gone astray a precious quarter of an hour was wasted, and the sun already hung, a dull red globe, on the brink of the horizon.

Clenching my teeth, I tore at my horse's flanks, and with a bloody heel I drove the maddened brute along at a pace that might have cost us both dearly. I dashed, at last, into the quadrangle, and, throwing the reins to a gaping groom, I sprang up the steps.

"Has the Chevalier returned?" I gasped breathlessly.

"Not yet, Monsieur," answered Guilbert with a tranquillity that made me desire to strangle him. "Is Mademoiselle in the château?" was my next question, mechanically asked.

"I saw her on the terrace some moments ago. She has not since come within."

Like one possessed I flew across the intervening room and out on to the terrace. Geneviève and Andrea were walking there, deep in conversation. At another time I might have cursed their lack of prudence. At the moment I did not so much as remark it.

"Where is Mademoiselle de Canaples?" I burst out.

They gazed at me, as much astounded by my question and the abruptness of it as by my apparent agitation.

Has anything happened?" inquired Geneviève, her blue eyes wide open.

"Yes—no; naught has happened. Tell me where she is. I must speak to her."

"She was here a while ago," said Andrea, "but she left us to stroll along the river bank."

"How long is it since she left you?"

"A quarter of an hour, perhaps."

"Something has happened!" cried Geneviève, and added more, maybe, but I waited not to hear.

Muttering curses as I ran—for 't was my way to curse where pious souls might pray—I sped back to the quadrangle and my horse.

"Follow me," I shouted to the groom, "you and as many of your fellows as you can find. Follow me at once—at once, mark you—to the coppice by the river." And without waiting for his answer, I sent my horse thundering down the avenue. The sun was gone, leaving naught but a roseate streak to tell of its passage, and at that moment a distant bell tinkled forth the Angelus.

With whip, spur, and imprecations I plied my steed, a prey to such excitement as I had never known until that moment—not even in the carnage of battle.

I had no plan. My mind was a chaos of thought without a single clear idea to light it, and I never so much as bethought me that single-handed I was about to attempt to wrest Yvonne from the hands of perchance half a dozen men. To save time I did not far pursue the road, but, clearing a hedge, I galloped ventre-à-terre across the meadow towards the little coppice by the waterside. As I rode I saw no sign of any moving thing. No sound disturbed the evening stillness save the dull thump of my horse's hoofs upon the turf, and a great fear arose in my heart that I might come too late.

At last I reached the belt of trees, and my fears grew into certainty. The place was deserted.

Then a fresh hope sprang up. Perchance, thinking of my warning, she had seen the emptiness of her suspicions towards me, and had pursued that walk of hers in another direction.

But when I had penetrated to the little open space within that cluster of naked trees, I had proof overwhelming that the worst had befallen. Not only on the moist ground was stamped the impress of struggling feet, but on a branch I found a strip of torn green velvet, and, remembering the dress she had worn that day, I understood to the full the significance of that rag, and, understanding it, I groaned aloud.

CHAPTER XII

THE RESCUE

Some precious moments did I waste standing with that green rag betwixt my fingers, and I grew sick and numb in body and in mind. She was gone! Carried off by a man I had reason to believe she hated, and whom God send she might have no motive to hate more deeply hereafter!

The ugly thought swelled until it blotted out all others, and in its train there came a fury upon me that drove me to do by instinct that which earlier I should have done by reason. I climbed back into the saddle, and away across the meadow I went, journeying at an angle with the road, my horse's head turned in the direction of Blois. That road at last was gained, and on I thundered at a stretched gallop, praying that my hard-used beast might last until the town was reached.

Now, as I have already said, I am not a man who easily falls a prey to excitement. It may have beset me in the heat of battle, when the fearsome lust of blood and death makes of every man a raving maniac, thrilled with mad joy at every stab he deals, and laughing with fierce passion at every blow he takes, though in the taking of it his course be run. But, saving at such wild times, never until then could I recall having been so little master of myself. There was a fever in me; all hell was in my blood, and, stranger still, and hitherto unknown at any season, there was a sickly fear that mastered me, and drew out great beads of sweat upon my brow. Fear for myself I have never known, for at no time has life so pampered me that the thought of parting company with it concerned me greatly. Fear for another I had not known till then—saving perchance the uneasiness that at times I had felt touching Andrea—because never yet had I sufficiefltly cared.

Thus far my thoughts took me, as I rode, and where I have halted did they halt, and stupidly I went over their ground again, like one who gropes for something in the dark,—because never yet had I sufficiently cared—I had never cared.

And then, ah Dieu! As I turned the thought over I understood, and, understanding, I pursued the sentence where I had left off.

But, caring at last, I was sick with fear of what might befall the one I cared for! There lay the reason of the frenzied excitement whereof I had become the slave. That it was that had brought the moisture to my brow and curses to my lips; that it was that had caused me instinctively to thrust the rag of green velvet within my doublet.

Ciel! It was strange—aye, monstrous strange, and a right good jest for fate to laugh at—that I, Gaston de Luynes, vile ruffler and worthless spadassin, should have come to such a pass; I, whose forefinger had for the past ten years uptilted the chin of every tavern wench I had chanced upon; I, whose lips had never known the touch of other than the lips of these; I, who had thought my heart long dead to tenderness and devotion, or to any fondness save the animal one for my ignoble self. Yet there I rode as if the Devil had me for a quarry,—panting, sweating, cursing, and well-nigh sobbing with rage at a fear that I might come too late,—all because of a proud lady who knew me for what I was and held me in contempt because of her knowledge; all for a lady who had not the kindness for me that one might spare a dog—who looked on me as something not good to see.

Since there was no one to whom I might tell my story that he might mock me, I mocked myself—with a laugh that startled passers-by and which, coupled with the crazy pace at which I dashed into Blois, caused them, I doubt not, to think me mad. Nor were they wrong, for mad indeed I deemed myself.

That I trampled no one underfoot in my furious progress through the streets is a miracle that passes my understanding.

In the courtyard of the Lys de France I drew rein at last with a tug that brought my shuddering brute on to his haunches and sent those who stood about flying into the shelter of the doorways.

"Another horse!" I shouted as I sprang to the ground. "Another horse at once!"

Then as I turned to inquire for Michelot, I espied him leaning stolidly against the portecochère.

"How long have you been there, Michelot?" I asked.

"Half an hour, mayhap."

"Saw you a closed carriage pass?"

"Ten minutes ago I saw one go by, followed by M. de St. Auban and a gentleman who greatly resembled M. de Vilmorin, besides an escort of four of the most villainous knaves—"

"That is the one," I broke in. "Quick, Michelot! Arm yourself and get your horse; I have need of you. Come, knave, move yourself!"

At the end of a few minutes we set out at a sharp trot, leaving the curious ones whom my loud-voiced commands had assembled, to speculate upon the meaning of so much bustle. Once clear of the township we gave the reins to our horses, and our trot became a gallop as we travelled along the road to Meung, with the Loire on our right. And as we went I briefly told Michelot what was afoot, interlarding my explanations with prayers that we might come upon the kidnappers before they crossed the river, and curses at the flying pace of our mounts, which to my anxious mind seemed slow.

At about a mile from Blois the road runs over an undulation of the ground that is almost a hill. From the moment that I had left Canaples as the Angelus was ringing, until the moment when our panting horses gained the brow of that little eminence, only half an hour had sped.

Still in that half-hour the tints had all but faded from the sky, and the twilight shadows grew thicker around us with every moment. Yet not so thick had they become but that I could see a coach at a standstill in the hollow, some three hundred yards beneath us, and, by it, half a dozen horses, of which four were riderless and held by the two men who were still mounted. Then, breathlessly scanning the field between the road and the river, I espied five persons, half way across, and at the same distance from the water that we were from the coach. Two men, whom I supposed to be St. Auban and Vilmorin, were forcing along a woman, whose struggles, feeble though they appeared—yet retarded their progress in some measure. Behind them walked two others, musket on shoulder.

I pointed them out to Michelot with a soft cry of joy. We were in time!

Following with my eyes the course they appeared to be pursuing I saw by the bank a boat, in which two men were waiting. Again I pointed, this time to the boat.

"Over the hedge, Michelot!" I cried. "We must ride in a straight line for the water and so intercept them. Follow me."

Over the hedge we went, and down the gentle slope at as round a pace as the soft ground would with safety allow. I had reckoned upon being opposed to six or even eight men, whereas there were but four, one of whom I knew was hardly to be reckoned. Doubtless St. Auban had imagined himself safe from pursuit when he left two of his bravos with the horses, probably to take them on to Meung, and there cross with them and rejoin him. Two more, I doubted not, were those seated at the oars.

I laughed to myself as I took in all this, but, even as I laughed, those in the field stood still, and sent up a shout that told me we had been perceived.

"On, Michelot, on!" I shouted, spurring my horse forward. Then, in answer to their master's call, the two ruffians who had been doing duty as grooms came pounding into the field.

"Ride to meet them, Michelot!" I cried. Obediently he wheeled to the left, and I caught the swish of his sword as it left the scabbard.

St. Auban was now hurrying towards the river with his party. Already they were but fifty yards from the boat, and a hundred still lay between him and me. Furiously I pressed onward, and presently but half the distance separated us, whilst they were still some thirty yards from their goal.

Then his two bravos faced round to meet me, and one, standing some fifty paces in advance of the other, levelled his musket and fired. But in his haste he aimed too high; the bullet carried away my hat, and before the smoke had cleared I was upon him. I had drawn a pistol from my holster, but it was not needed; my horse passed over him before he could save himself from my fearful charge.

In the fast-fading light a second musket barrel shone, and I saw the second ruffian taking aim at me with not a dozen yards between us. With the old soldier's instinct I wrenched at the reins till I brought my horse on to his haunches. It was high time, for simultaneously with my action the fellow blazed at me, and the scream of pain that broke from my steed told me that the poor brute had taken the bullet. With a bound that carried me forward some six paces, the animal sank, quivering, to the ground. I disengaged my feet from the stirrups as he fell, but the shock of it sent me rolling on the ground, and the ruffian, seeing me fallen, sprang forward, swinging his musket up above his head. I dodged the murderous downward stroke, and as the stock buried itself close beside me in the soft earth I rose on one knee and with a grim laugh I raised my pistol. I brought the muzzle within a hand's breadth of his face, then fired and shot him through the head. Perchance you'll say it was a murderous, cruel stroke: mayhap it was, but at such seasons men stay not to unravel niceties, but strike ere they themselves be stricken.

Leaping over the twitching corpse, I got out my sword and sprang after St. Auban, who, with Vilmorin and Yvonne, careless of what might betide his followers, was now within ten paces of the boat.

Pistol shots cracked behind me, and I wondered how Michelot was faring, but dared not pause to look.

The twain in the boat stood up, wielding their great oars, and methought them on the point of coming to their master's aid, in which case my battle had truly been a lost one. But that craven Vilmorin did me good service then, for with a cry of fear at my approach, he abandoned his hold of Yvonne, whose struggles were keeping both the men back; thus freed, he fled towards the boat, and jumping in, he shouted to the men in his shrill, quavering voice, to put off. Albeit they disobeyed him contemptuously and waited for the Marquis; still they did not leave the boat, fearing, no doubt, that if they did so the coward would put off alone.

As for St. Auban, Vilmorin's flight left him unequal to the task of dragging the girl along. She dug her heels into the ground, and, tug as he might, for all that he set both hands to work, he could not move her. In this plight I came upon him, and challenged him to stand and face me.

With a bunch of oaths he got out his sword, but in doing so he was forced to remove one of his hands from the girl's arm. Seizing the opportunity with a ready wit and courage seldom found in women of her quality, she twisted herself from the grip of his left hand, and came staggering towards me for protection, holding up her pinioned wrists. With my blade I severed the cord, whereupon she plucked the gag from her mouth, and sank against my side, her struggles having left her weak indeed.

As I set my arm about her waist to support her, my heart seemed to swell within me, and strange melodies shaped themselves within my soul.

St. Auban bore down upon me with a raucous oath, but the glittering point of my rapier danced before his eyes and drove him back again.

"To me, Vilmorin, you cowardly cur!" he shouted. "To me, you dogs!"

He let fly at them a volley of blood-curdling oaths, then, without waiting to see if they obeyed him, he came at me again, and our swords met.

"Courage, Mademoiselle," I whispered, as a sigh that was almost a groan escaped her. "Have no fear."

But that fight was not destined to be fought, for, as again we engaged, there came the fall of running feet behind me. It flashed across my mind that Michelot had been worsted, and that my back was about to be assailed. But in St. Auban's face I saw, as in a mirror, that he who came was Michelot.

"Mort de Christ!" snarled the Marquis, springing back beyond my reach. "What can a man do with naught but fools and poltroons to serve him? Faugh! We will continue our sword-play at St. Sulpice des Reaux tonight. Au revoir, M. de Luynes!"

Turning, he sheathed his sword, and, running down to the river, bounded into the boat, where I heard him reviling Vilmorin with every foul name he could call to mind.

My blood was aflame, and I was not minded to wait for our meeting at Reaux. Consigning Mademoiselle to the care of Michelot, who stood panting and bleeding from a wound in his shoulder, I turned back to my dead horse, and plucking the remaining pistol from the holster I ran down to the very edge of the water. The boat was not ten yards from shore, and my action had been unheeded by St. Auban, who was standing in the stern.

Kneeling I took careful aim at him, and as God lives, I would have saved much trouble that was to follow had I been allowed to fire. But at that moment a hand was laid upon my arm, and Yvonne's sweet voice murmured in my ear:

"You have fought a brave and gallant fight, M. de Luynes, and you have done a deed of which the knights of old might have been proud. Do not mar it by an act of murder."

"Murder, Mademoiselle!" I gasped, letting my hand fall. "Surely there is no murder in this!"

"A suspicion of it, I think, and so brave a man should have clean hands."

CHAPTER XIII

THE HAND OF YVONNE

We did not long remain upon the field of battle. Indeed, if we lingered at all it was but so that Mademoiselle might bandage Michelot's wound. And whilst she did so, my stout henchman related to us how it had fared with him, and how, having taken the two ruffians separately, he had been wounded by the first, whom he repaid by splitting his skull, whereupon the second one had discharged his pistol without effect, then made off towards the road, whilst Michelot, remembering that I might need assistance, had let him go.

"There, good Michelot," quoth Mademoiselle, completing her task, "I have done what little I can. And now, M. de Luynes, let us go."

It was close upon seven o'clock, and night was at hand. Already the moon was showing her large, full face above the tree-tops by Chambord, and casting a silver streak athwart the stream. The plash of oars from the Marquis's boat was waxing indistinct despite the stillness, whilst by the eye the boat itself was no longer to be distinguished.

As I turned, my glance fell upon the bravo whom I had shot. He lay stiff and stark upon his back, his sightless eyes wide open and staring heavenwards, his face all blood-smeared and ghastly to behold.

Mademoiselle shuddered. "Let us go," she repeated in a faint whisper; her eye had also fallen on that thing, and her voice was full of awe. She laid her hand upon my sleeve and 'neath the suasion of her touch I moved away.

To our surprise and joy we found St. Auban's coach where we had left it, with two saddled horses tethered close by. The others had doubtless been taken by the coachman and the bravo who had escaped Michelot, both of whom had fled. These animals we looked upon as the spoils of war, and accordingly when we set out in the coach,—Mademoiselle having desired me to ride beside her therein,—Michelot wielding the reins, it was with those two horses tethered behind.

"Monsieur de Luynes," said my companion softly, "I fear that I have done you a great injustice. Indeed, I know not how to crave your forgiveness, how to thank you, or how to hide my shame at those words I spoke to you this afternoon at Canaples."

"Not another word on that score, Mademoiselle!"

And to myself I thought of what recompense already had been mine. To me it had been given to have her lean trustingly upon me, my arm about her waist, whilst, sword in hand, I had fought for her. Dieu! Was that not something to have lived for?—aye, and to have died for, methought.

"I deserved, Monsieur," she continued presently, "that you should have left me to my fate for all the odious things I uttered when you warned me of my peril,—for the manner in which I have treated you since your coming to Blois."

"You have but treated me, Mademoiselle, in the only manner in which you could treat one so far beneath you, one who is utterly unworthy that you should bestow a single regret upon him."

"You are strangely humble tonight, Monsieur. It is unwonted in you, and for once you wrong yourself. You have not said that I am forgiven."

"I have naught to forgive."

"Hélas! you have—indeed you have!"

"Eh, bien!" quoth I, with a return of my old tone of banter, "I forgive then."

Thereafter we travelled on in silence for some little while, my heart full of joy at being so near to her, and the friendliness which she evinced for me, and my mind casting o'er my joyous heart a cloud of some indefinable evil presage.

"You are a brave man, M. de Luynes," she murmured presently, "and I have been taught that brave men are ever honourable and true."

"Had they who taught you that known Gaston de Luynes, they would have told you instead that it is possible for a vile man to have the one redeeming virtue of courage, even as it is possible for a liar to have a countenance that is sweet and innocent."

"There speaks that humble mood you are affecting, and which sits upon you as my father's clothes might do. Nay, Monsieur, I shall believe in my first teaching, and be deaf to yours."

Again there was a spell of silence. At last—"I have been thinking, Monsieur," she said, "of that other occasion on which you rode with me. I remember that you said you had killed a man, and when I asked you why, you said that you had done it because he sought to kill you. Was that the truth?"

"Assuredly, Mademoiselle. We fought a duel, and it is customary in a duel for each to seek to kill the other."

"But why was this duel fought?" she cried, with some petulance.

"I fear me, Mademoiselle, that I may not answer you," I said, recalling the exact motives, and thinking how futile appeared the quarrel which Eugène de Canaples had sought with Andrea when viewed in the light of what had since befallen.

"Was the quarrel of your seeking?"

"In a measure it was, Mademoiselle."

"In a measure!" she echoed. Then persisting, as women will—"Will you not tell me what this measure was?"

"Tenez, Mademoiselle," I answered in despair; "I will tell you just so much as I may. Your brother had occasion to be opposed to certain projects that were being formed in Paris by persons high in power around a beardless boy. Himself of too small importance to dare wage war against those powerful ones who would have crushed him, your brother sought to gain his ends by sending a challenge to this boy. The lad was high-spirited and consented to meet M. de Canaples, by whom he would assuredly have been murdered—'t is the only word, Mademoiselle—had I not intervened as I did."

She was silent for a moment. Then—"I believe you, Monsieur," she said simply. "You fought, then, to shield another—but why?"

"For three reasons, Mademoiselle. Firstly, those persons high in power chose to think it my fault that the quarrel had arisen, and threatened to hang me if the duel took place and the boy were harmed. Secondly, I myself felt a kindness for the boy. Thirdly, because, whatever sins Heaven may record against me, it has at least ever been my way to side against men who, confident of their superiority, seek, with the cowardly courage of the strong, to harm the weak. It is, Mademoiselle, the courage of the man who knows no fear when he strikes a woman, yet who will shake with a palsy when another man but threatens him."

"Why did you not tell me all this before?" she whispered, after a pause. And methought I caught a quaver in her voice.

I laughed for answer, and she read my laugh aright; presently she pursued her questions and asked me the name of the boy I had defended. But I evaded her, telling her that she must need no further details to believe me.

"It is not that, Monsieur! I do believe you; I do indeed, but—"

"Hark, Mademoiselle!" I cried suddenly, as the clatter of many hoofs sounded near at hand. "What is that?"

A shout rang out at that moment. "Halt! Who goes there?"

"Mon Dieu!" exclaimed Mademoiselle, drawing close up to me, and again the voice sounded, this time more sinister.

"Halt, I say—in the King's name!"

The coach came to a standstill, and through the window I beheld the shadowy forms of several mounted men, and the feeble glare of a lantern.

"Who travels in the carriage, knave?" came the voice again.

"Mademoiselle de Canaples," answered Michelot; then, like a fool, he must needs add: "Have a care whom you knave, my master, if you would grow old."

"Pardieu! let us behold this Mademoiselle de Canaples who owns so fearful a warrior for a coachman."

The door was flung rudely open, and the man bearing the lantern—whose rays shone upon a uniform of the Cardinal's guards—confronted us.

With a chuckle he flashed the light in my face, then suddenly grew serious.

"Peste! Is it indeed you, M. de Luynes?" quoth he; adding, with stern politeness, "It grieves me to disturb you, but I have a warrant for your arrest."

He was fumbling in his doublet as he spoke, and during the time I had leisure to scan his countenance, recognising, to my surprise, a young lieutenant of the guards who had but recently served with me, and with whom I had been on terms almost of friendship. His words, "I have a warrant for your arrest," came like a bolt from the blue to enlighten me, and to remind me of what St. Auban had that morning told me, and which for the nonce I had all but forgotten.

Upon hearing those same words, Yvonne, methought, grew pale, and her eyes were bent upon me with a look of surprise and pity.

"Upon what charge am I arrested?" I enquired, with forced composure.

"My warrant mentions none, M. de Luynes. It is here." And he thrust before me a paper, whose purport I could have read in its shape and seals. Idly my eye ran along the words:

"By these presents I charge and empower my lieutenant, Jean de Montrésor, to seize where'er he may be found, hold, and conduct to Paris the Sieur Gaston de Luynes—"

And so further, until the Cardinal's signature ended the legal verbiage.

"In the King's name, M. de Luynes," said Montrésor, firmly yet deferentially, "your sword!"

It would have been madness to do aught but comply with his request, and so I surrendered my rapier, which he in his turn delivered to one of his followers. Next I stepped down from the coach and turned to take leave of Mademoiselle, whereupon Montrésor, thinking that peradventure matters were as they appeared to be between us, and, being a man of fine feelings, signed to his men to fall back, whilst he himself withdrew a few paces.

"Adieu, Mademoiselle!" I said simply. "I shall carry with me for consolation the memory that I have been of service to you, and I shall ever—during the little time that may be left me—be grateful to Heaven for the opportunity that it has afforded me of causing you—perchance without sufficient reason—to think better of me. Adieu, Mademoiselle! God guard you!"

It was too dark to see her face, but my heart bounded with joy to catch in her voice a quaver that argued, methought, regret for me.

"What does it mean, M. de Luynes? Why are they taking you?"

"Because I have displeased my Lord Cardinal, albeit, Mademoiselle, I swear to you that I have no cause for shame at the reasons for which I am being arrested."

"My father is Monseigneur de Mazarin's friend," she cried. "He is also yours. He shall exert for you what influence he possesses."

"'T were useless, Mademoiselle. Besides, what does it signify? Again, adieu!"

She spoke no answering word, but silently held out her hand. Silently I took it in mine, and for a moment I hesitated, thinking of what I was—of what she was. At last, moved by some power that was greater than my will, I stooped and pressed those shapely fingers to my lips. Then I stepped suddenly back and closed the carriage door, oppressed by a feeling akin to that of having done an evil deed.

"Have I your permission to say a word to my servant, M. le Lieutenant?" I inquired.

106

He bowed assent, whereat, stepping close up to the horror-stricken Michelot—

"Drive straight to the Château de Canaples," I said in a low voice. "Thereafter return to the Lys de France and there wait until you hear from me. Here, take my purse; there are some fifty pistoles in it."

"Speak but the word, Monsieur," he growled, "and I'll pistol a couple of these dogs."

"Pah! You grow childish," I laughed, "or can you not see that fellow's musket?"

"Pardieu! I'll risk his aim! I never yet saw one of these curs shoot straight."

"No, no, obey me, Michelot. Think of Mademoiselle. Go! Adieu! If we should not meet again, mon brave," I finished, as I seized his loyal hand, "what few things of mine are at the hostelry shall belong to you, as well as what may be left of this money. It is little enough payment, Michelot, for all your faithfulness—"

"Monsieur, Monsieur!" he cried.

"Diable!" I muttered, "we are becoming women! Be off, you knave! Adieu!"

The peremptoriness of my tone ended our leave-taking and caused him to grip his reins and bring down his whip. The coach moved on. A white face, on which the moonlight fell, glanced at me from the window, then to my staring eyes naught was left but the back of the retreating vehicle, with one of the two saddle-horses that had been tethered to it still ambling in its wake.

"M. de Montrésor," I said, thrusting my bullet-pierced hat upon my head, "I am at your service."

CHAPTER XIV

OF WHAT BEFELL AT REAUX

At my captor's bidding I mounted the horse which they had untethered from the carriage, and we started off along the road which the coach itself had disappeared upon a moment before. But we travelled at a gentle trot, which, after that evening's furious riding, was welcome to me.

With bitterness I reflected as I rode that the very moment at which Mademoiselle de Canaples had brought herself to think better of me was like to prove the last we should spend together. Yet not altogether bitter was that reflection; for with it came also the consolation—whereof I had told her—that I had not been taken before she had had cause to change her mind concerning me.

That she should care for me was too preposterous an idea to be nourished, and, indeed, it was better—much better—that M. de Montrésor had come before I, grown sanguine as lovers will, had again earned her scorn by showing her what my heart contained. Much better was it that I should pass for ever out of her life—as, indeed, methought I was like to pass out of all life—whilst I could leave in her mind a kind remembrance and a grateful regret, free from the stain that a subsequent possible presumption of mine might have cast o'er it.

Then my thoughts shifted to Andrea. St. Auban would hear of my removal, and I cared not to think of what profit he might derive from it. To Yvonne also his presence must hereafter be a menace, and in that wherein tonight he had failed, he might, again, succeed. It was at this juncture of my reverie that M. de Montrésor's pleasant young voice aroused me.

"You appear downcast, M. de Luynes."

"I, downcast!" I echoed, throwing back my head and laughing. "Nay. I was but thinking.

"Believe me, M. de Luynes," he said kindly, "when I tell you that it grieves me to be charged with this matter. I have done my best to capture you. That was my duty. But I should have rejoiced had I failed with the consciousness of having done all in my power."

"Thanks, Montrésor," I murmured, and silence followed.

"I have been thinking, Monsieur," he went on presently, "that possibly the absence of your sword causes you discomfort."

"Eh? Discomfort? It does, most damnably!"

"Give me your parole d'honneur that you will attempt no escape, and not only shall your sword be returned to you, but you shall travel to Paris with all comfort and dignity."

Now, so amazed was I that I paused to stare at the officer who was young enough to make such a proposal to a man of my reputation. He turned his face towards me, and in the moonlight I could make out his questioning glance.

"Eh, bien, Monsieur?"

"I am more than grateful to you, M. de Montrésor," I replied, "and I freely give you my word of honour to seek no means of eluding you, nor to avail myself of any that may be presented to me."

I said this loud enough for those behind to hear, so that no surprise was evinced when the lieutenant bade the man who bore my sword return it to me.

If he who may chance to read these simple pages shall have gathered aught of my character from their perusal, he will marvel, perchance, that I should give the lieutenant my parole, instead rather of watching for an opportunity to—at least—attempt an escape. Preeminent in my thoughts, however, stood at that moment the necessity to remove St.

Auban, and methought that by acting as I did I saw a way by which, haply, I might accomplish this. What might thereafter befall me seemed of little moment.

"M. de Montrésor," I said presently, "your kindness impels me to set a further tax upon your generosity."

"That is, Monsieur?"

"Bid your men fall back a little, and I will tell you."

He made a sign to his troopers, and when the distance between us had been sufficiently widened, I began:

"There is a man at present across the river, yonder, who has done me no little injury, and with whom I have a rendezvous at nine o'clock tonight at St. Sulpice des Reaux, where our swords are to determine the difference between us. I crave, Monsieur, your permission to keep that appointment."

"Impossible!" he answered curtly.

I took a deep breath like a man who is about to jump an obstacle in his path.

"Why impossible, Monsieur?"

"Because you are a prisoner, and therefore no longer under obligation to keep appointments."

"How would you feel, Montrésor, if, burning to be avenged upon a man who had done you irreparable wrong, you were arrested an hour before the time at which you were to meet this man, sword in hand, and your captor—whose leave you craved to keep the assignation—answered you with the word 'impossible'?"

"Yes, yes, Monsieur," he replied impatiently. "But you forget my position. Let us suppose that I allow you to go to St. Sulpice des Reaux. What if you do not return?"

"You mistrust me?" I exclaimed, my hopes melting.

"You misapprehend me. I mean, what if you are killed?"

"I do not think that I shall be."

"Ah! But what if you are? What shall I say to my Lord Cardinal?"

110

"Dame! That I am dead, and that he is saved the trouble of hanging me. The most he can want of me is my life. Let us suppose that you had come an hour later. You would have been forced to wait until after the encounter, and, did I fall, matters would be no different."

The young man fell to thinking, but I, knowing that it is not well to let the young ponder overlong if you would bend them to your wishes, broke in upon his reflections—"See, Montrésor, yonder are the lights of Blois; by eight o'clock we shall be in the town. Come; grant me leave to cross the Loire, and by ten o'clock, or half-past at the latest, I shall return to sup with you or I shall be dead. I swear it."

"Were I in your position," he answered musingly, "I know how I would be treated, and, pardieu! come what may I shall deal with you accordingly. You may go to your assignation, M. de Luynes, and may God prosper you."

And thus it came to pass that shortly after eight o'clock, albeit a prisoner, I rode into the courtyard of the Lys de France, and, alighting, I stepped across the threshold of the inn, and strode up to a table at which I had espied Michelot. He sat nursing a huge measure of wine, into the depths of which he was gazing pensively, with an expression so glum upon his weather-beaten countenance that it defies depicting. So deep was he in his meditations, that albeit I stood by the table surveying him for a full minute, he took no heed of me.

"Allons, Michelot!" I said at length. "Wake up."

He started up with a cry of amazement; surprise chased away the grief that had been on his face, and a moment later joy unfeigned, and good to see, took the place of surprise.

"You have escaped, Monsieur!" he cried, and albeit caution made him utter the words beneath his breath, a shout seemed to lurk somewhere in the whisper.

Pressing his hand I sat down and briefly told him how matters stood, and how I came to be for the moment free. And when I had done I bade him, since his wound had not proved serious, to get his hat and cloak and go with me to find a boat.

He obeyed me, and a quarter of an hour after we had quitted the hostelry he was rowing me across the stream, whilst, wrapped in my cloak, I sat in the stern, thinking of Yvonne.

"Monsieur," said Michelot, "observe how swift is the stream. If I were to let the boat drift we should be at Tours tomorrow, and from there it would be easy to defy pursuit. We have enough money to reach Spain. What say you, Monsieur?"

"Say, you rascal? Why, bend your back to the work and set me ashore by St. Sulpice in a quarter of an hour, or I'll forget that you have been my friend. Would you see me dishonoured?"

"Sooner than see you dead," he grumbled as he resumed his task. Thereafter, whilst he rowed, Michelot entertained me with some quaint ideas touching that which fine gentlemen call honour, and to what sorry passes it was wont to bring them, concluding by thanking God that he was no gentleman and had no honour to lead him into mischief.

At last, however, our journey came to an end, and I sprang ashore some five hundred paces from the little chapel, and almost exactly opposite the Château de Canaples. I stood for a moment gazing across the water at the lighted windows of the château, wondering which of those eyes that looked out upon the night might be that of Yvonne's chamber.

Then, bidding Michelot await me, or follow did I not return in half an hour, I turned and moved away towards the chapel.

There is a clearing in front of the little white edifice—which rather than a temple is but a monument to the martyr who is said to have perished on that spot in the days before Clovis.

As I advanced into the centre of this open patch of ground, and stood clear of the black silhouettes of the trees, cast about me by the moon, two men appeared to detach themselves from the side wall of the chapel, and advanced to meet me.

Albeit they were wrapped in their cloaks—uptilted behind by their protruding scabbards—it was not difficult to tell the tall figure and stately bearing of St. Auban and the mincing gait of Vilmorin.

I doffed my hat in a grave salutation, which was courteously returned.

"I trust, Messieurs, that I have not kept you waiting?"

"I was on the point of expressing that very hope, Monsieur," returned St. Auban. "We have but arrived. Do you come alone?"

"As you perceive."

"Hum! M. le Vicomte, then, will act for both of us."

I bowed in token of my satisfaction, and without more ado cast aside my cloak, pleased to see that the affair was to be conducted with decency and politeness, as such matters should ever be conducted, albeit impoliteness may have marked their origin.

The Marquis, having followed my example and divested himself of his cloak and hat, unsheathed his rapier and delivered it to Vilmorin, who came across with it to where I stood. When he was close to me I saw that he was deadly pale; his teeth chattered, and the hand that held the weapon shook as with a palsy.

"Mu—Monsieur," he stammered, "will it please you to lend me your sword that I may mu-measure it?"

"What formalities!" I exclaimed with an amused smile, as I complied with his request. "I am afraid you have caught a chill, Vicomte. The night air is little suited to health so delicate."

He answered me with a baleful glance, as silently he took my sword and set it—point to hilt—with St. Auban's. He appeared to have found some slight difference in the length, for he took two steps away from me, holding the weapons well in the light, where for a moment he surveyed them attentively. His hands shook so that the blades clattered one against the other the while. But, of a sudden, taking both rapiers by the hilt, he struck the blades together with a ringing clash, then flung them both behind him as far as he could contrive, leaving me thunderstruck with amazement, and marvelling whether fear had robbed him of his wits.

Not until I perceived that the trees around me appeared to spring into life did it occur to me that that clashing of blades was a signal, and that I was trapped. With the realisation of it I was upon Vilmorin in a bound, and with both hands I had caught the dog by the throat before he thought of flight. The violence of my onslaught bore him to the ground, and I, not to release my choking grip, went with him.

For a moment we lay together where we had fallen, his slender body twisting and writhing under me, his swelling face upturned and his protruding, horror-stricken eyes gazing into mine that were fierce and pitiless. Voices rang above me; someone stooped and strove to pluck me from my victim; then below the left shoulder I felt a sting of pain, first cold then hot, and I knew that I had been stabbed.

Again I felt the blade thrust in, lower down and driven deeper; then, as the knife was for the second time withdrawn, and my flesh sucked at the steel,—the pain of it sending a shudder through me,—the instinct of preservation overcame the sweet lust to strangle Vilmorin. I let him go and, staggering to my feet, I turned to face those murderers who struck a defenceless man behind.

Swords gleamed around me: one, two, three, four, five, six, I counted, and stood weak and dazed from loss of blood, gazing stupidly at the white blades. Had I but had my sword I should have laid about me, and gone down beneath their blows as befits a soldier. But the absence of that trusty friend left me limp and helpless—cowed for the first time since I had borne arms.

Of a sudden I became aware that St. Auban stood opposite to me, hand on hip, surveying me with a malicious leer. As our eyes met—"So, master meddler," quoth he mockingly, "you crow less lustily than is your wont."

"Hound!" I gasped, choking with rage, "if you are a man, if there be a spark of pride or honour left in your lying, cowardly soul, order your

114

assassins to give me my sword, and, wounded though I be, I'll fight with you this duel that you lured me here to fight."

He laughed harshly.

"I told you but this morning, Master de Luynes, that a St. Auban does not fight men of your stamp. You forced a rendezvous upon me; you shall reap the consequences."

Despite the weakness arising from loss of blood, I sprang towards him, beside myself with fury. But ere I had covered half the distance that lay between us my arms were gripped from behind, and in my spent condition I was held there, powerless, at the Marquis's mercy. He came slowly forward until we were but some two feet apart. For a second he stood leering at me, then, raising his hand, he struck me—struck a man whose arms another held!—full upon the face. Passion for the moment lent me strength, and in that moment I had wrenched my right arm free and returned his blow with interest.

With an oath he got out a dagger that hung from his baldrick.

"Sang du Christ! Take that, you dog!" he snarled, burying the blade in my breast as he spoke.

"My God! You are murdering me!" I gasped.

"Have you discovered it? What penetration!" he retorted, and those about him laughed at his indecent jest!

He made a sign, and the man who had held me withdrew his hands. I staggered forward, deprived of his support, then a crashing blow took me across the head.

I swayed for an instant, and with arms upheld I clutched at the air, as if I sought, by hanging to it, to save myself from falling; then the moon appeared to go dark, a noise as of the sea beating upon its shore filled my ears, and I seemed to be falling—falling—falling.

A voice that buzzed and vibrated oddly, growing more distant at each word, reached me as I sank.

"Come," it said. "Fling that carrion into the river."

Then nothingness engulfed me.

CHAPTER XV

OF MY RESURRECTION

Even as the blow which had plunged me into senselessness had imparted to me the sinking sensation which I have feebly endeavoured to depict, so did the first dim ray of returning consciousness bring with it the feeling that I was again being buoyed upwards through the thick waters that had enveloped me, to their surface, where intelligence and wakefulness awaited.

And as I felt myself borne up and up in that effortless ascension, my senses awake and my reason still half-dormant, an exquisite sense of languor pervaded my whole being. Presently meseemed that the surface was gained at last, and an instinct impelled me to open my eyes upon the light, of which, through closed lids, I had become conscious.

I beheld a fair-sized room superbly furnished, and flooded with amber sunlight suggestive in itself of warmth and luxury, the vision of which heightened the delicious torpor that held me in thrall. The bed I lay upon was such, I told myself, as would not have disgraced a royal sleeper. It was upheld by great pillars of black oak, carved with a score of fantastic figures, and all around it, descending from the dome above, hung curtains of rich damask, drawn back at the side that looked upon the window. Near at hand stood a table laden with phials and such utensils as one sees by the bedside of the wealthy sick. All this I beheld in a languid, unreasoning fashion through my half-open lids, and albeit the luxury of the room and the fine linen of my bed told me that this was neither my Paris lodging in the Rue St. Antoine, nor yet my chamber at the hostelry of the Lys de France, still I taxed not my brain with any questions touching my whereabouts.

I closed my eyes, and I must have slept again: when next I opened them a burly figure stood in the deep bay of the latticed window, looking out through the leaded panes.

I recognised the stalwart frame of Michelot, and at last I asked myself where I might be. It did not seem to occur to me that I had but to call him to receive an answer to that question. Instead, I closed my eyes again, and essayed to think. But just then there came a gentle scratching at the door, and I could hear Michelot tiptoeing across the room; next he and the one he had admitted tiptoed back towards my bedside, and as they came I caught a whisper in a voice that seemed to drag me to full consciousness.

"How fares the poor invalid this morning?"

"The fever is gone, Mademoiselle, and he may wake at any moment; indeed, it is strange that he should sleep so long."

"He will be the better for it when he does awaken. I will remain here while you rest, Michelot. My poor fellow, you are almost as worn with your vigils as he is with the fever."

"Pooh! I am strong enough, Mademoiselle," he answered. "I will get a mouthful of food and return, for I would be by when he wakes."

Then their voices sank so low that as they withdrew I caught not what was said. The door closed softly and for a space there was silence, broken at last by a sigh above my head. With an answering sigh I opened wide my eyes and feasted them upon the lovely face of Yvonne de Canaples, as she bent over me with a look of tenderness and pity that at once recalled to me our parting when I was arrested.

But suddenly meeting the stare of my gaze, she drew back with a half-stifled cry, whose meaning my dull wits sought not to interpret, but methought I caught from her lips the words, "Thank God!"

"Where am I, Mademoiselle?" I inquired, and the faintness of my voice amazed me.

"You know me!" she exclaimed, as though the thing were a miracle. Then coming forward again, and setting her cool, sweet hand upon my forehead,

"Hush," she murmured in the accents one might use to soothe a child. "You are at Canaples, among friends. Now sleep."

"At Canaples!" I echoed. "How came I here? I am a prisoner, am I not?"

"A prisoner!" she exclaimed. "No, no, you are not a prisoner. You are among friends."

"Did I then but dream that Montrésor arrested me yesterday on the road to Meung? Ah! I recollect! M. de Montrésor gave me leave on parole to go to Reaux."

Then, like an avalanche, remembrance swept down upon me, and my memory drew a vivid picture of the happenings at St. Sulpice.

"My God!" I cried. "Am I not dead, then?" And I sought to struggle up into a sitting posture, but that gentle hand upon my forehead restrained and robbed me of all will that was not hers.

"Hush, Monsieur!" she said softly. "Lie still. By a miracle and the faithfulness of Michelot you live. Be thankful, be content, and sleep."

"But my wounds, Mademoiselle?" I inquired feebly.

"They are healed."

"Healed?" quoth I, and in my amazement my voice sounded louder than it had yet done since my awakening. "Healed! Three such wounds as I took last night, to say naught of a broken head, healed?"

"'T was not last night, Monsieur."

"Not last night? Was it not last night that I went to Reaux?"

"It is nearly a month since that took place," she answered with a smile. "For nearly a month have you lain unconscious upon that bed, with the angel of Death at your pillow. You have fought and won a silent battle. Now sleep, Monsieur, and ask no more questions until next you awaken, when Michelot shall tell you all that took place."

She held a glass to my lips from which I drank gratefully, then, with the submissiveness of a babe, I obeyed her and slept.

As she had promised, it was Michelot who greeted me when next I opened my eyes, on the following day. There were tears in his eyes—eyes that had looked grim and unmoved upon the horrors of the battlefield.

From him I learned how, after they had flung me into the river, deeming me dead already, St. Auban and his men had made off. The swift stream swirled me along towards the spot where, in the boat, Michelot awaited my return all unconscious of what was taking place. He had heard the splash, and had suddenly stood up, on the point of going ashore, when my body rose within a few feet of him. He spoke of the agony of mind wherewith he had suddenly stretched forth and clutched me by my doublet, fearing that I was indeed dead. He had lifted me into the boat to find that my heart still beat and that the blood flowed from my wounds. These he had there and then bound up in the only rude fashion he was master of, and forthwith, thinking of Andrea and the Chevalier de Canaples, who were my friends, and of Mademoiselle, who was my debtor, also seeing that the château was the nearest place, he had rowed straight across to Canaples, and there I had lain during the four weeks that had elapsed, nursed by Mademoiselle, Andrea, and himself, and thus won back to life.

Ah, Dieu! How good it was to know that someone there was still who cared for worthless Gaston de Luynes a little—enough to watch beside him and withhold his soul from the grim claws of Death.

"What of M. de St. Auban?" I inquired presently.

"He has not been seen since that night. Probably he feared that did he come to Blois, the Chevalier would find means of punishing him for the attempted abduction of Mademoiselle."

"Ah, then Andrea is safe?"

As if in answer to my question, the lad entered at that moment, and upon seeing me sitting up, talking to Michelot, he uttered an exclamation of joy, and hurried forward to my bedside.

"Gaston, dear friend!" he cried, as he took my hand—and a thin, withered hand it was.

We talked long together,—we three,—and anon we were joined by the Chevalier de Canaples, who offered me also, in his hesitating manner, his felicitations. And with me they lingered until Yvonne came to drive them with protestations from my bedside.

Such, in brief, was the manner of my resurrection. For a week or so I still kept my chamber; then one day towards the middle of April, the weather being warm and the sun bright, Michelot assisted me to don my clothes, which hung strangely empty upon my gaunt, emaciated frame, and, leaning heavily upon my faithful henchman, I made my way below.

In the salon I found the Chevalier de Canaples with Mesdemoiselles and Andrea awaiting me, and the kindness wherewith they overwhelmed me, as I sat propped up with pillows, was such that I asked myself again and again if, indeed, I was that same Gaston de Luynes who but a little while ago had held himself as destitute of friends as he was of fortune. I was the pampered hero of the hour, and even little Geneviève had a sunny smile and a kind word for me.

Thereafter my recovery progressed with great strides, and gradually, day by day, I felt more like my old vigorous self. They were happy days, for Mademoiselle was often at my side, and ever kind to me; so kind was she that presently, as my strength grew, there fell a great cloud athwart my happiness—the thought that soon I must leave Canaples never to return there,—leave Mademoiselle's presence never to come into it again.

I was Monsieur de Montrésor's prisoner. I had learned that in common with all others, save those at Canaples, he deemed me dead, and that, informed of it by a message from St. Auban, he had returned to Paris on the day following that of my journey to Reaux. Nevertheless, since I lived, he had my parole, and it was my duty as soon as I had regained sufficient strength, to journey to Paris and deliver myself into his hands.

Nearer and nearer drew the dreaded hour in which I felt that I must leave Canaples. On the last day of April I essayed a fencing bout with Andrea, and so strong and supple did I prove myself that I was forced to realise that the time was come. On the morrow I would go.

As I was on the point of returning indoors with the foils under my arm, Andrea called me back.

"Gaston, I have something of importance to say to you. Will you take a turn with me down yonder by the river?"

There was a serious, almost nervous look on his comely face, which arrested my attention. I dropped the foils, and taking his arm I went with him as he bade me. We seated ourselves on the grass by the edge of the gurgling waters, and he began:

"It is now two months since we came to Blois: I, to pay my court to the wealthy Mademoiselle de Canaples; you, to watch over and protect me—nay, you need not interrupt me. Michelot has told me what St. Auban sought here, and the true motives of your journey to St. Sulpice. Never shall I be able to sufficiently prove my gratitude to you, my poor Gaston. But tell me, dear friend, you who from the outset saw how matters stood, why did you not inform St. Auban that he had no cause to hunt me down since I intended not to come between him and Yvonne?"

"Mon Dieu!" I exclaimed, "that little fair-haired coquette has—"

"Gaston," he interrupted, "you go too fast. I love Geneviève de Canaples. I have loved her, I think, since the moment I beheld her in the inn at Choisy, and, what is more, she loves me."

"So that—?" I asked with an ill-repressed sneer.

"We have plighted our troth, and with her father's sanction, or without it, she will do me the honour to become my wife."

"Admirable!" I exclaimed. "And my Lord Cardinal?"

"May hang himself on his stole for aught I care."

"Ah! Truly a dutiful expression for a nephew who has thwarted his uncle's plans!"

"My uncle's plans are like himself, cold and selfish in their ambition."

"Andrea, Andrea! Whatever your uncle may be, to those of your blood, at least, he was never selfish."

"Not selfish!" he cried. "Think you that he is enriching and contracting great alliances for us because he loves us? No, no. Our uncle seeks to gain our support and with it the support of those noble houses to which he is allying us. The nobility opposes him, therefore he seeks to find relatives among noblemen, so that he may weather the storm of which his far-seeing eyes have already detected the first dim clouds. What to him are my feelings, my inclinations, my affections? Things of no moment, to be sacrificed so that I may serve him in the manner that will bring him the most profit. Yet you call him not selfish! Were he not selfish, I should go to him and say: 'I love Geneviève de Canaples. Create me Duke as you would do, did I wed her sister, and the Chevalier de Canaples will not withstand our union.' What think you would be his answer?"

"I have a shrewd idea what his answer would be," I replied slowly. "Also I have a shrewd idea of what he will say when he learns in what manner you have defied his wishes."

"He can but order me away from Court, or, at most, banish me from France."

"And then what will become of you—of you and your wife?"

"What is to become of us?" he cried in a tone that was almost that of anger. "Think you that I am a pauper dependent upon my uncle's bounty? I have an estate near Palermo, which, for all that it does not yield riches, is yet sufficient to enable us to live with dignity and comfort. I have told Geneviève, and she is content."

I looked at his flushed face and laughed.

"Well, well!" said I. "If you are resolved upon it, it is ended."

He appeared to meditate for a moment, then—"We have decided to be married by the Curé of St. Innocent on the day after tomorrow."

"Crédieu!" I answered, with a whistle, "you have wasted no time in determining your plans. Does Yvonne know of it?"

"We have dared tell nobody," he replied; and a moment later he added hesitatingly, "You, I know, will not betray us."

"Do you know me so little that you doubt me on that score? Have no fear, Andrea, I shall not speak. Besides, tomorrow, or the next day at latest, I leave Canaples."

122

"You do not mean that you are returning to the Lys de France!"

"No. I am going farther than that. I am going to Paris."

"To Paris?"

"To Paris, to deliver myself up to M. de Montrésor, who gave me leave to go to Reaux some seven weeks ago."

"But it is madness, Gaston!" he ejaculated.

"All virtue is madness in a world so sinful; nevertheless I go. In a measure I am glad that things have fallen out with you as they have done, for when the news goes abroad that you have married Geneviève de Canaples and left the heiress free, your enemies will vanish, and you will have no further need of me. New enemies you will have perchance, but in your strife with them I could lend you no help, were I by."

He sat in silence casting pebbles into the stream, and watching the ripples they made upon the face of the waters.

"Have you told Mademoiselle?" he asked at length.

"Not yet. I shall tell her today. You also, Andrea, must take her into your confidence touching your approaching marriage. That she will prove a good friend to you I am assured."

"But what reason shall I give form my secrecy?" he inquired, and inwardly I smiled to see how the selfishness which love begets in us had caused him already to forget my affairs, and how the thought of his own approaching union effaced all thought of me and the doom to which I went.

"Give no reason," I answered. "Let Genevieve tell her of what you contemplate, and if a reason she must have, let Geneviève bid her come to me. This much will I do for you in the matter; indeed, Andrea, it is the last service I am like to render you."

"Sh! Here comes the Chevalier. She shall be told today."

CHAPTER XVI

THE WAY OF WOMAN

For all that I realised that this love of mine for Yvonne was as a child still-born—a thing that had no existence save in the heart that had begotten it—I rejoiced meanly at the thought that she was not destined to become Andrea's wife. For since I understood that this woman—who to me was like no other of her sex—was not for so poor a thing as Gaston de Luynes, like the dog in the fable I wished that no other might possess her. Inevitable it seemed that sooner or later one must come who would woo and win her. But ere that befell, my Lord Cardinal would have meted out justice to me—the justice of the rope meseemed—and I should not be by to gnash my teeth in jealousy.

That evening, when the Chevalier de Canaples had gone to pay a visit to his vineyard,—the thing that, next to himself, he loved most in this world,—and whilst Geneviève and Andrea were vowing a deathless love to each other in the rose garden, their favourite haunt when the Chevalier was absent, I seized the opportunity for making my adieux to Yvonne.

We were leaning together upon the balustrade of the terrace, and our faces were turned towards the river and the wooded shores beyond—a landscape this that was as alive and beautiful now as it had been dead and grey when first I came to Canaples two months ago.

Scarce were my first words spoken when she turned towards me, and methought—but I was mad, I told myself—that there was a catch in her voice as she exclaimed, "You are leaving us, Monsieur?"

"Tomorrow morning I shall crave Monsieur your father's permission to quit Canaples."

"But why, Monsieur? Have we not made you happy here?"

"So happy, Mademoiselle," I answered with fervour, "that at times it passes my belief that I am indeed Gaston de Luynes. But go I must. My honour demands of me this sacrifice."

And in answer to the look of astonishment that filled her wondrous eyes, I told her what I had told Andrea touching my parole to Montrésor, and the necessity of its redemption. As Andrea had done, she also dubbed it madness, but her glance was, nevertheless, so full of admiration, that methought to have earned it was worth the immolation of liberty—of life perchance; who could say?

"Before I go, Mademoiselle," I pursued, looking straight before me as I spoke, and dimly conscious that her glance was bent upon my face—"before I go, I fain would thank you for all that you have done for me here. Your care has saved my life, Mademoiselle; your kindness, methinks, has saved my soul. For it seems to me that I am no longer the same man whom Michelot fished out of the Loire that night two months ago. I would thank you, Mademoiselle, for the happiness that has been mine during the past few days—a happiness such as for years has not fallen to my lot. To another and worthier man, the task of thanking you might be an easy one; but to me, who know myself to be so far beneath you, the obligation is so overwhelming that I know of no words to fitly express it."

"Monsieur, Monsieur, I beseech you! Already you have said overmuch."

"Nay, Mademoiselle; not half enough."

"Have you forgotten, then, what you did for me? Our trivial service to you is but unseemly recompense. What other man would have come to my rescue as you came, with such odds against you—and forgetting the affronting words wherewith that very day I had met your warning? Tell me, Monsieur, who would have done that?"

"Why, any man who deemed himself a gentleman, and who possessed such knowledge as I had."

She laughed a laugh of unbelief.

"You are mistaken, sir," she answered. "The deed was worthy of one of those preux chevaliers we read of, and I have never known but one man capable of accomplishing it."

Those words and the tone wherein they were uttered set my brain on fire. I turned towards her; our glances met, and her eyes—those eyes that but a while ago had never looked on me without avowing the disdain wherein she had held me—were now filled with a light of kindliness, of sympathy, of tenderness that seemed more than I could endure.

Already my hand was thrust into the bosom of my doublet, and my fingers were about to drag forth that little shred of green velvet that I had found in the coppice on the day of her abduction, and that I had kept ever since as one keeps the relic of a departed saint. Another moment and I should have poured out the story of the mad, hopeless passion that filled my heart to bursting, when of a sudden—"Yvonne, Yvonne!" came Geneviève's fresh voice from the other end of the terrace. The spell of that moment was broken.

Methought Mademoiselle made a little gesture of impatience as she answered her sister's call; then, with a word of apology, she left me.

Half dazed by the emotions that had made sport of me, I leaned over the balustrade, and with my elbows on the stone and my chin on my palms, I stared stupidly before me, thanking God for having sent Geneviève in time to save me from again earning Mademoiselle's scorn. For as I grew sober I did not doubt that with scorn she would have met the wild words that already trembled on my lips.

I laughed harshly and aloud, such a laugh as those in Hell may vent. "Gaston, Gaston!" I muttered, "at thirty-two you are more a fool than ever you were at twenty."

I told myself then that my fancy had vested her tone and look with a kindliness far beyond that which they contained, and as I thought of how I had deemed impatient the little gesture wherewith she had greeted Geneviève's interruption I laughed again.

From the reverie into which, naturally enough, I lapsed, it was Mademoiselle who aroused me. She stood beside me with an unrest of manner so unusual in her, that straightway I guessed the substance of her talk with Geneviève.

"So, Mademoiselle," I said, without waiting for her to speak, "you have learned what is afoot?"

"I have," she answered. "That they love each other is no news to me. That they intend to wed does not surprise me. But that they should contemplate a secret marriage passes my comprehension."

I cleared my throat as men will when about to embark upon a perilous subject with no starting-point determined.

"It is time, Mademoiselle," I began, "that you should learn the true cause of M. de Mancini's presence at Canaples. It will enlighten you touching his motives for a secret wedding. Had things fallen out as was intended by those who planned his visit—Monsieur your father and my Lord Cardinal—it is improbable that you would ever have heard that which it now becomes necessary that I should tell you. I trust, Mademoiselle," I continued, "that you will hear me in a neutral spirit, without permitting your personal feelings to enter into your consideration of that which I shall unfold."

"So long a preface augurs anything but well," she interposed, looking monstrous serious.

"Not ill, at least, I hope. Hear me then. Your father and his Eminence are friends; the one has a daughter who is said to be very wealthy and whom he, with fond ambition, desires to see wedded to a man who can give her an illustrious name; the other possesses a nephew whom he can ennoble by the highest title that a man may bear who is not a prince of the blood,—and borne indeed by few who are not,—and whom he desires to see contract an alliance that will bring him enough of riches to enable him to bear his title with becoming dignity." I glanced at Mademoiselle, whose cheeks were growing an ominous red.

"Well, Mademoiselle," I continued, "your father and Monseigneur de Mazarin appear to have bared their heart's desire to each other, and M. de Mancini was sent to Canaples to woo and win your father's elder daughter."

A long pause followed, during which she stood with face aflame, averted eyes, and heaving bosom, betraying the feelings that stormed within her at the disclosure of the bargain whereof she had been a part. At length—"Oh, Monsieur!" she exclaimed in a choking voice, and clenching her shapely hands, "to think—"

"I beseech you not to think, Mademoiselle," I interrupted calmly, for, having taken the first plunge, I was now master of myself. "The ironical little god, whom the ancients painted with bandaged eyes, has led M. de Mancini by the nose in this matter, and things have gone awry for the plotters. There, Mademoiselle, you have the reason for a clandestine union. Did Monsieur your father guess how Andrea's affections have"— I caught the word "miscarried" betimes, and substituted—"gone against his wishes, his opposition is not a thing to be doubted."

"Are you sure there is no mistake?" she inquired after a pause. "Is all this really true, Monsieur?"

"It is, indeed."

"But how comes it that my father has seen naught of what has been so plain to me—that M. de Mancini was ever at my sister's side?"

"Your father, Mademoiselle, is much engrossed in his vineyard. Moreover, when the Chevalier has been at hand he has been careful to show no greater regard for the one than for the other of you. I instructed him in this duplicity many weeks ago."

She looked at me for a moment.

"Oh, Monsieur," she cried passionately, "how deep is my humiliation! To think that I was made a part of so vile a bargain! Oh, I am glad that M. de Mancini has proved above the sordid task to which they set him—glad that he will dupe the Cardinal and my father."

"So am not I, Mademoiselle," I exclaimed. She vouchsafed me a stare of ineffable surprise.

"How?

"Diable!" I answered. "I am M. de Mancini's friend. It was to shield him that I fought your brother; again, because of my attitude towards him was it that I went perilously near assassination at Reaux. Enemies sprang up about him when the Cardinal's matrimonial projects became known. Your brother picked a quarrel with him, and when I had dealt with your brother, St. Auban appeared, and after St. Auban there were others. When it is known that he has played this trick upon 'Uncle Giulio' his enemies will disappear; but, on the other hand, his prospects will all be blighted, and for that I am sorry."

"So that was the motive of your duel with Eugène!"

"At last you learn it."

"And," she added in a curious voice, "you would have been better pleased had M. de Mancini carried out his uncle's wishes?"

"It matters little what I would think, Mademoiselle," I answered guardedly, for I could not read that curious tone of hers.

"Nevertheless, I am curious to hear your answer."

What answer could I make? The truth—that for all my fine talk, I was at heart and in a sense right glad that she was not to become Andrea's wife—would have seemed ungallant. Moreover, I must have added the explanation that I desired to see her no man's wife, so that I might not seem to contradict myself. Therefore—

"In truth, Mademoiselle," I answered, lying glibly, "it would have given me more pleasure had Andrea chosen to obey his Eminence."

Her manner froze upon the instant.

"In the consideration of your friend's advancement," she replied, half contemptuously, "you forget, M. de Luynes, to consider me. Am I, then, a thing to be bartered into the hands of the first fortune-hunter who woos me because he has been bidden so to do, and who is to marry me for political purposes? Pshaw, M. de Luynes!" she added, with a scornful laugh, "after all, I was a fool to expect aught else from—"

She checked herself abruptly, and a sudden access of mercy left the stinging "you" unuttered. I stood by, dumb and sheepish, not understanding how the words that I had deemed gallant could have brought this tempest down upon my head. Before I could say aught that might have righted matters, or perchance made them worse—"Since you leave Canaples tomorrow," quoth she, "I will say 'Adieu,' Monsieur, for it is unlikely that we shall meet again."

With a slight inclination of her head, and withholding her hand intentionally, she moved away, whilst I stood, as only a fool or a statue would stand, and watched her go.

Once she paused, and, indeed, half turned, whereupon hope knocked at my heart again; but before I had admitted it, she had resumed her walk towards the house. Hungrily I followed her graceful, lissom figure with my eyes until she had crossed the threshold. Then, with a dull ache in my breast, I flung myself upon a stone seat, and, addressing myself to the setting sun for want of a better audience, I roundly cursed her sex for the knottiest puzzle that had ever plagued the mind of man in the unravelling.

CHAPTER XVII

FATHER AND SON

"Gaston," quoth Andrea next morning, "you will remain at Canaples until tomorrow? You must, for tomorrow I am to be wed, and I would fain have your good wishes ere you go."

"Nice hands, mine, to seek a benediction at," I grumbled.

"But you will remain? Come, Gaston, we have been good friends, you and I, and who knows when next we shall meet? Believe me, I shall value your 'God speed' above all others."

"Likely enough, since it will be the only one you'll hear."

But for all my sneers he was not to be put off. He talked and coaxed so winningly that in the end—albeit I am a man not easily turned from the course he has set himself—the affectionate pleading in his fresh young voice and the affectionate look in his dark eyes won me to his way.

Forthwith I went in quest of the Chevalier, whom, at the indication of a lackey, I discovered in the room it pleased him to call his study—that same room into which we had been ushered on the day of our arrival at Canaples. I told him that on the morrow I must set out for Paris, and albeit he at first expressed a polite regret, yet when I had shown him how my honour was involved in my speedy return thither, he did not urge me to put off my departure.

"It grieves me, sir, that you must go, and I deeply regret the motive that is taking you. Yet I hope that his Eminence, in recognition of the services you have rendered his nephew, will see fit to forget what cause for resentment he may have against you, and render you your liberty. If you will give me leave, Monsieur, I will write to his Eminence in this strain, and you shall be the bearer of my letter."

I thanked him, with a smile of deprecation, as I thought of the true cause of Mazarin's resentment, which was precisely that of the plea upon which M. de Canaples sought to obtain for me my liberation.

"And now, Monsieur," he pursued nervously, "touching Andrea and his visit here, I would say a word to you who are his friend, and may haply know something of his mind. It is over two months since he came here, and yet the—er—affair which we had hoped to bring about seems no nearer its conclusion than when first he came. Of late I have watched him and I have watched Yvonne; they are certainly good friends, yet not even the frail barrier of formality appears overcome betwixt them, and I am beginning to fear that Andrea is not only lukewarm in this matter, but is forgetful of his uncle's wishes and selfishly indifferent to Monseigneur's projects and mine, which, as he well knows, are the reason of his sojourn at my château. What think you of this, M. de Luynes?"

He shot a furtive glance at me as he spoke, and with his long, lean forefinger he combed his beard in a nervous fashion.

I gave a short laugh to cover my embarrassment at the question.

"What do I think, Monsieur?" I echoed to gain time. Then, thinking that a sententious answer would be the most fitting,—"Ma foi! Love is as the spark that lies latent in flint and steel: for days and weeks these two may be as close together as you please, and naught will come of it; but one fine day, a hand—the hand of chance—will strike the one against the other, and lo!—the spark is born!"

"You speak in parables, Monsieur," was his caustic comment.

"'T is in parables that all religions are preached," I returned, "and love, methinks, is a great religion in this world."

"Love, sir, love!" he cried petulantly. "The word makes me sick! What has love to do with this union? Love, sir, is a pretty theme for poets, romancers, and fools. The imagination of such a sentiment—for it is a

132

sentiment that does not live save in the imagination—may serve to draw peasants and other lowbred clods into wedlock. With such as we—with gentlemen—it has naught to do. So let that be, Monsieur. Andrea de Mancini came hither to wed my daughter."

"And I am certain, Monsieur," I answered stoutly, "that Andrea will wed your daughter."

"You speak with confidence."

"I know Andrea well. Signs that may be hidden to you are clear to me, and I have faith in my prophecy."

He looked at me, and fell a victim to my confidence of manner. The petulancy died out of his face.

"Well, well! We will hope. My Lord Cardinal is to create him Duke, and he will assume as title his wife's estate, becoming known to history as Andrea de Mancini, Duke of Canaples. Thus shall a great house be founded that will bear our name. You see the importance of it?"

"Clearly."

"And how reasonable is my anxiety?"

"Assuredly."

"And you are in sympathy with me?"

"Pardieu! Why else did I go so near to killing your son?"

"True," he mused. Then suddenly he added, "Apropos, have you heard that Eugène has become one of the leaders of these frondeur madmen?"

"Ah! Then he is quite recovered?"

"Unfortunately," he assented with a grimace, and thus our interview ended.

That day wore slowly to its close. I wandered hither and thither in the château and the grounds, hungering throughout the long hours for a word with Mademoiselle—a glimpse of her, at least.

But all day long she kept her chamber, the pretext being that she was beset by a migraine. By accident I came upon her that evening, at last, in the salon; yet my advent was the signal for her departure, and all the words she had for me were:

"Still at Canaples, Monsieur? I thought you were to have left this morning."
She looked paler than her wont, and her eyes were somewhat red.

"I am remaining until tomorrow," said I awkwardly.

"Vraiement!" was all she answered, and she was gone.

Next morning the Chevalier and I breakfasted alone. Mademoiselle's migraine was worse. Geneviève was nursing, so her maid brought word— whilst Andrea had gone out an hour before and had not returned.

The Chevalier shot me an apologetic glance across the board.

"'T is a poor 'God speed' to you, M. de Luynes."

I made light of it and turned the conversation into an indifferent channel, wherein it abided until, filling himself a bumper of Anjou, the Chevalier solemnly drank to my safe journey and good fortune in Paris.

At that moment Andrea entered by the door abutting on the terrace balcony. He was flushed, and his eyes sparkled with a joyous fever. Profuse was he in his apologies, which, howbeit, were passing vague in character, and which he brought to a close by pledging me as the Chevalier had done already.

As we rose, Geneviève appeared with the news that Yvonne was somewhat better, adding that she had come to take leave of me. Her composure surprised me gladly, for albeit in her eyes there was also a telltale light, the lids, demurely downcast as was her wont, amply screened it from the vulgar gaze.

Andrea would tell his father-in-law of the marriage later in the day; and for all I am not a chicken-hearted man, still I had no stomach to be at hand when the storm broke.

The moment having come for my departure, and Michelot awaiting me already with the horses in the courtyard, M. de Canaples left us to seek the letter which I was to carry to his Eminence. So soon as the door had closed upon him, Andrea came forward, leading his bride by the hand, and asked me to wish them happiness.

"With all my heart," I answered; "and if happiness be accorded you in a measure with the fervency of my wishes then shall you, indeed, be happy. Each of you I congratulate upon the companion in life you have chosen. Cherish him, Mademoi—Madame, for he is loyal and true—and such are rare in this world."

It is possible that I might have said more in this benign and fatherly strain—for it seemed to me that this new role I had assumed suited me wondrous well—but a shadow that drew our eyes towards the nearest window interrupted me. And what we saw there drew a cry from Andrea, a shudder from Geneviève, and from me a gasp that was half amazement, half dismay. For, leaning upon the sill, surveying us with a sardonic, evil grin, we beheld Eugène de Canaples, the man whom I had left with a sword-thrust through his middle behind the Hôtel Vendôme two months ago. Whence was he sprung, and why came he thus to his father's house?

He started as I faced him, for doubtless St. Auban had boasted to him that he had killed me in a duel. For a moment he remained at the window, then he disappeared, and we could hear the ring of his spurred heel as he walked along the balcony towards the door.

And simultaneously came the quick, hurrying steps of the Chevalier de Canaples, as he crossed the hall, returning with the letter he had gone to fetch.

Geneviève shuddered again, and looked fearfully from one door to the other; Andrea drew a sharp breath like a man in pain, whilst I rapped out an oath to brace my nerves for the scene which we all three foresaw. Then in silence we waited, some subtle instinct warning us of the disaster that impended.

The steps on the balcony halted, and a second later those in the hall; and then, as though the thing had been rehearsed and timed so that the spectators might derive the utmost effect from it, the doors opened together, and on the opposing thresholds, with the width of the room betwixt them, stood father and son confronted.

CHAPTER XVIII

OF HOW I LEFT CANAPLES

Whilst a man might tell a dozen did those two remain motionless, the one eyeing the other. But their bearing was as widely different as their figures; Eugène's stalwart frame stood firm and erect, insolence in every line of it, reflected perchance from the smile that lurked about the corners of his thinlipped mouth.

The hat, which he had not had the grace to doff, set jauntily upon his straight black hair, the jerkin of leather which he wore, and the stout sword which hung from the plainest of belts, all served to give him the air of a ruffler, or tavern knight.

The Chevalier, on the other hand, stood as if turned to stone. From his enervated fingers the letter fluttered to the ground, and on his pale, thin face was to be read a displeasure mixed with fear.

At length, with an oath, the old man broke the silence.

"What seek you at Canaples?" he asked in a quivering voice, as he advanced into the room. "Are you so dead to shame that you dare present yourself with such effrontery? Off with your hat, sir!" he blazed, stamping his foot, and going from pale to crimson. "Off with your hat, or Mortdieu, I'll have you flung out of doors by my grooms."

This show of vehemence, as sudden as it was unexpected, drew from Eugène a meek obedience that I had not looked for. Nevertheless, the young man's lip curled as he uncovered.

"How fatherly is your greeting!" he sneered. The Chevalier's eyes flashed a glance that lacked no venom at his son.

"What manner of greeting did you look for?" he returned hotly. "Did you expect me to set a ring upon your finger, and have the fattened calf killed in honour of your return? Sangdieu, sir! Have you come hither to show me how a father should welcome the profligate son who has dishonoured his name? Why are you here, unbidden? Answer me, sir!"

A deep flush overspread Eugène's cheeks.

"I had thought when I crossed the threshold that this was the Château de Canaples, or else that my name was Canaples—I know not which. Clearly I was mistaken, for here is a lady who has no word either of greeting or intercession for me, and who, therefore, cannot be my sister, and yonder a man whom I should never look to find in my father's house."

I took a step forward, a hot answer on my lips, when from the doorway at my back came Yvonne's sweet voice.

"Eugène! You here?"

"As you see, Sister. Though had you delayed your coming 't is probable you would no longer have found me, for your father welcomes me with oaths and threatens me with his grooms."

She cast a reproachful glance upon the Chevalier, 'neath which the anger seemed to die out of him; then she went forward with hands outstretched and a sad smile upon her lips.

"Yvonne!" The Chevalier's voice rang out sharp and sudden.

She stopped.

"I forbid you to approach that man!"

For a moment she appeared to hesitate; then, leisurely pursuing her way, she set her hands upon her brother's shoulders and embraced him.

The Chevalier swore through set teeth; Geneviève trembled, Andrea looked askance, and I laughed softly at the Chevalier's discomfiture.

Eugène flung his hat and cloak into a corner and strode across the room to where his father stood.

"And now, Monsieur, since I have travelled all the way from Paris to save my house from a step that will bring it into the contempt of all France, I shall not go until you have heard me."

The Chevalier shrugged his shoulders and made as if to turn away. Yvonne's greeting of her brother appeared to have quenched the spark of spirit that for a moment had glimmered in the little man's breast.

"Monsieur," cried Eugène, "believe me that what I have to say is of the utmost consequence, and say it I will—whether before these strangers or in your private ear shall be as you elect."

The old man glanced about him like one who seeks a way of escape. At last—"If say it you must," he growled, "say it here and now. And when you have said it, go."

Eugène scowled at me, and from me to Andrea. To pay him for that scowl, I had it in my mind to stay; but, overcoming the clownish thought, I took Andrea by the arm.

"Come, Andrea," I said, "we will take a turn outside while these family matters are in discussion."

I had a shrewd idea what was the substance of Eugène's mission to Canaples—to expostulate with his father touching the proposed marriage of Yvonne to the Cardinal's nephew.

Nor was I wrong, for when, some moments later, the Chevalier recalled us from the terrace, where we were strolling—"What think you he has come hither to tell me?" he inquired as we entered. He pointed to his son as he spoke, and passion shook his slender frame as the breeze shakes a leaf. Mademoiselle and Geneviève sat hand in hand—Yvonne deadly pale, Geneviève weeping.

"What think you he has the effrontery to say? Têtedieu! it seems that he has profited little by the lesson you read him in the horse-market about meddling in matters which concern him not. He has come hither to tell me that he will not permit his sister to wed the Cardinal's nephew;

that he will not have the estates of Canaples pass into the hands of a foreign upstart. He, forsooth—he! he! he!" And at each utterance of the pronoun he lunged with his forefinger in the direction of his son. "This he is not ashamed to utter before Yvonne herself!"

"You compelled me to do so," cried Eugène angrily.

"I?" ejaculated the Chevalier. "Did I compel you to come hither with your 'I will' and 'I will not'? Who are you, that you should give laws at Canaples? And he adds, sir," quoth the old knight excitedly, "that sooner than allow this marriage to take place he will kill M. de Mancini."

"I shall be happy to afford him the opportunity!" shouted Andrea, bounding forward.

Eugène looked up quickly and gave a short laugh. Thereupon followed a wild hubbub; everyone rushed forward and everyone talked; even little Geneviève—louder than all the rest.

"You shall not fight! You shall not fight!" she cried, and her voice was so laden with command that all others grew silent and all eyes were turned upon her.

"What affair is this of yours, little one?" quoth Eugène.

"'T is this," she answered, panting, "that you need fear no marriage 'twixt my sister and Andrea."

In her eagerness she had cast caution to the winds of heaven. Her father and brother stared askance at her; I gave an inward groan.

"Andrea!" echoed Eugène at last. "What is this man to you that you speak thus of him?"

The girl flung herself upon her father's breast.

"Father," she sobbed, "dear father, forgive!"

The Chevalier's brow grew dark; roughly he seized her by the arms and, holding her at arm's length, scanned her face.

"What must I forgive?" he inquired in a thick voice. "What is M. de Mancini to you?"

Some sinister note in her father's voice caused the girl to grow of a sudden calm and to assume a rigidity that reminded me of her sister.

"He is my husband!" she answered. And there was a note of pride—almost of triumph—in her voice.

An awful silence followed the launching of that thunderbolt. Eugène stood with open mouth, staring now at Geneviève, now at his father. Andrea set his arm about his bride's waist, and her fair head was laid trustingly upon his shoulder. The Chevalier's eyes rolled ominously. At length he spoke in a dangerously calm voice.

"How long is it—how long have you been wed?"

"We were wed in Blois an hour ago," answered Geneviève.

Something that was like a grunt escaped the Chevalier, then his eye fastened upon me, and his anger boiled up.

"You knew of this?" he asked, coming towards me.

"I knew of it."

"Then you lied to me yesterday."

I drew myself up, stiff as a broomstick.

"I do not understand," I answered coldly.

"Did you not give me your assurance that M. de Mancini would marry Yvonne?"

"I did not, Monsieur. I did but tell you that he would wed your daughter. And, ma foi! your daughter he has wed."

"You have fooled me, scélérat!" he blazed out. "You, who have been sheltered by—"

"Father!" Yvonne interrupted, taking his arm. "M. de Luynes has behaved no worse than have I, or any one of us, in this matter."

"No!" he cried, and pointed to Andrea. "'T is you who have wrought this infamy. Eugène," he exclaimed, turning of a sudden to his son, "you have a sword; wipe out this shame."

"Shame!" echoed Geneviève. "Oh, father, where is the shame? If it were no shame for Andrea to marry Yvonne, surely—"

"Silence!" he thundered. "Eugène—"

But Eugène answered him with a contemptuous laugh.

"You are quick enough to call upon my sword, now that things have not fallen out as you would have them. Where are your grooms now, Monsieur?"

"Insolent hound!" cried his father indignantly. Then, letting fall his arms with something that was near akin to a sob—"Is there no one left to do aught but mock me?" he groaned.

But this weakness was no more than momentary.

"Out of my house, sir!" he blazed, turning upon Andrea, and for a moment methought he would have struck him. "Out of my house—you and this wife of yours!"

"Father!" sobbed Geneviève, with hands outstretched in entreaty.

"Out of my house," he repeated, "and you also, M. de Luynes. Away with you! Go with the master you have served so well." And, turning on his heel, he strode towards the door.

"Father—dear father!" cried Geneviève, following him: he slammed the door in her face for answer.

With a moan she sank down upon her knees, her frail body shaken by convulsive sobs—Dieu! what a bridal morn was hers!

Andrea and Yvonne raised her and led her to a chair. Eugène watched them with a cynical eye, then laughed brutally, and, gathering up his hat and cloak, he moved towards the balcony door and vanished.

"Is M. de Luynes still there?" quoth Geneviève presently.

"I am here, Madame."

"You had best set out, Monsieur," she said. "We shall follow soon— very soon."

I took Andrea aside and asked him whither it was his intention to take his wife. He replied that they would go to Chambord, where they would remain for some weeks in the hope that the Chevalier might relent sufficiently to forgive them. Thereafter it was his purpose to take his bride home to his Sicilian demesne.

Our farewells were soon spoken; yet none the less warm, for all its brevity, was my leave-taking of Andrea, and our wishes for each other's happiness were as fervent as the human heart can shape. We little thought that we were not destined to meet again for years.

Yvonne's adieu was cold and formal—so cold and formal that it seemed to rob the sunshine of its glory for me as I stepped out into the open air.

After all, what mattered it? I was a fool to have entertained a single tender thought concerning her.

CHAPTER XIX

OF MY RETURN TO PARIS

Scant cause is there for me to tarry over the details of my return to Paris. A sad enough journey was it; as sad for my poor Michelot as for myself, since he rode with one so dejected as I.

Things had gone ill, and I feared that when the Cardinal heard the story things would go worse, for Mazarin was never a tolerant man, nor one to be led by the gospel of mercy and forgiveness. For myself I foresaw the rope—possibly even the wheel; and a hundred times a day I dubbed myself a fool for obeying the voice of honour with such punctiliousness when so grim a reward awaited me. What mood was on me—me, Gaston de Luynes, whose honour had been long since besmirched and tattered until no outward semblance of honour was left?

But swift in the footsteps of that question would come the answer— Yvonne. Ay, truly enough, it was because in my heart I had dared to hold a sentiment of love for her, the purest—nay, the only pure—thing my heart had held for many a year, that I would set nothing vile to keep company with that sentiment; that until my sun should set—and already it dropped swiftly towards life's horizon—my actions should be the actions of such a man as might win Yvonne's affections.

But let that be. This idle restrospective mood can interest you but little; nor can you profit from it, unless, indeed, it be by noting how holy and cleansing to the heart of man is the love—albeit unrequited—that he bears a good woman.

As we drew near Meung—where we lay on that first night of our journey—a light travelling chaise, going in the same direction, passed us at a gallop. As it flashed by, I caught a glimpse of Eugène de Canaples's swart face through the window. Whether the recognition was mutual I cannot say—nor does it signify.

When we reached the Hôtel de la Couronne, half an hour later, we saw that same chaise disappearing round a corner of the street, whilst through the porte-cochère the hostler was leading a pair of horses, foam-flecked and steaming with sweat.

Whither went Master Canaples at such a rate, and in a haste that caused him to travel day and night? To a goal he little looked for—or rather, which, in the madness of his headlong rush, he could not see. So I was to learn ere long.

Next day I awoke betimes, and setting my window wide to let in the fresh, clean-smelling air of that May morning I made shift to dress. Save for the cackle of the poultry which had strayed into the courtyard, and the noisy yawns and sleep-laden ejaculations of the stable-boy, who was drawing water for the horses, all was still, for it had not yet gone five o'clock.

But of a sudden a door opened somewhere, and a step rang out, accompanied by the jangle of spurs, and with it came a sharp, unpleasant voice calling for its owner's horse. There was a familiar sound in those shrill accents that caused me to thrust my head through the casement. But I was quick to withdraw it, as I recognised in the gaily dressed little fellow below my old friend Malpertuis.

I know not what impulse made me draw back so suddenly. The action was as much the child of instinct as of the lately acquired habit of concealing my face from the gaze of all who were likely to spread abroad the news that I still lived.

From behind my curtains I watched Malpertuis ride out of the yard, saying, in answer to a parting question of the landlord, who had come upon the scene, that he would breakfast at Beaugency.

Then, as he rode down the street, he of a sudden raised his discordant voice and sang to the accompaniment of his horse's hoofs. And the burden of his song ran thus:

A frondeur wind
Got up today,
'Gainst Mazarin
It blows, they say.

I listened in amazement to his raven's voice.

Whither was he bound, I asked myself, and whence a haste that made him set out fasting, with an anti-cardinalist ditty on his lips, and ride two leagues to seek a breakfast in a village that did not hold an inn where a dog might be housed in comfort?

Like Eugène de Canaples, he also travelled towards a goal that he little dreamt of. And so albeit the one went south and the other north, these two men were, between them, drawing together the thread of this narrative of mine, as anon you shall learn.

We reached Paris at dusk three days later, and we went straight to my old lodging in the Rue St. Antoine.

Coupri started and gasped upon beholding me, and not until I had cursed him for a fool in a voice that was passing human would he believe that I was no ghost. He too had heard the rumour of my death.

I dispatched Michelot to the Palais Royal, where—without permitting his motive to transpire—he was to ascertain for me whether M. de Montrésor was in Paris, whether he still dwelt at the Hôtel des Cloches, and at what hour he could be found there.

Whilst he was away I went up to my room, and there I found a letter which Coupri informed me had been left by a lackey a month ago—before the report that I had been killed had reached Paris—and since lain forgotten. It was a delicate note, to which still hung the ghost of a perfume; there were no arms on the seal, but the writing I took to be that

145

of my aunt, the Duchesse de Chevreuse, and vaguely marvelling what motive she could have had for communicating with me, I cut the silk.

It was, indeed, from the Duchesse, but it contained no more than a request that I should visit her at her hôtel on the day following upon that on which she had written, adding that she had pleasing news for me.

I thrust the note into my pocket with a sigh. Of what could it avail me now to present myself at her hôtel? Her invitation was for a month ago. Since then she would likely enough have heard the rumour that had been current, and would have ceased to expect me.

I caught myself wondering whether the news might have caused her a pang of regret, and somehow methought this possible. For of all my relatives, Madame de Chevreuse was the only one—and she was but my aunt by marriage—who of late years had shown me any kindness, or even recognition. I marvelled what her pleasing news could be, and I concluded that probably she had heard of my difficulties, and wished once again to help me out of them. Well, my purse was hollow, indeed, at the moment, but I need not trouble her, since I was going somewhere where purses are not needed—on a journey to which no expenses are attached.

In my heart, nevertheless, I blessed the gracious lady, who, for all the lies that the world may have told of her, was the kindest woman I had known, and the best—save one other.

I was still musing when Michelot returned with the information that M. de Montrésor was to be found at the Hôtel des Cloches, whither he had gone to sup a few minutes before. Straightway I set out, bidding him attend me, and, muffled in my cloak, I proceeded at a brisk pace to the Rue des Fosses St. Germain, where the lieutenant's auberge was situated.

I left Michelot in the common-room, and, preceded by the plump little woman who owned the house, I ascended to Montrésor's chamber. I found the young soldier at table, and, fortunately, alone. He rose as I entered, and as the hostess, retreating, closed the door, I doffed my hat, and letting fall my cloak revealed myself. His lips parted, and I heard the hiss of an indrawn breath as his astonished eyes fell upon my countenance. My laugh dispelled his doubts that I might be other than flesh and blood—yet not his doubts touching my identity. He caught up a taper and, coming forward, he cast the light on my face for a moment, then setting the candle back upon the table, he vented his surprise in an oath or two, which was natural enough in one of his calling.

"'T is clear, Lieutenant," quoth I, as I detached my sword from the baldrick, "that you believed me dead. Fate willed, however, that I should be restored to life, and so soon as I had recovered sufficient strength to undertake the journey to Paris, I set out. I arrived an hour ago, and here I am, to redeem my word of honour, and surrender the sword and liberty which you but lent me."

I placed my rapier on the table and waited for him to speak. Instead, however, he continued to stare at me for some moments, and when at last he did break the silence, it was to burst into a laugh that poured from his throat in rich, mellow peals, as he lay back in his chair.

My wrath arose. Had I travelled from Blois, and done what I deemed the most honourable deed of my life, to be laughed at for my pains by a foppish young jackanapes of his Eminence's guards? Something of my displeasure must he have seen reflected on my face, for of a sudden he checked his mirth.

"Forgive me, M. de Luynes," he gasped. "Pardieu, 't is no matter for laughter, and albeit I laughed with more zest than courtesy, I give you my word that my admiration for you vastly exceeds my amusement. M. de Luynes," he added, rising and holding out his hand to me, "there are liars in Paris who give you an evil name—men who laughed at me when they heard that I had given you leave to go on parole to St. Sulpice des Reaux that night, trusting to your word of honour that you would return if you lived. His Eminence dubbed me a fool and went near to dismissing me from his service, and yet I have now the proof that my confidence was not misplaced, since even though you were believed to be dead, you did not hesitate to bring me your sword."

"Monsieur, spare me!" I exclaimed, for in truth his compliments waxed as irksome as had been his whilom merriment.

He continued, however, his laudatory address, and when it was at last ended, and he paused exhausted alike in breath and brain, it was to take up my sword and return it to me with my parole, pronouncing me a free man, and advising me to let men continue to think me dead, and to withdraw from France. He cut short my half-protesting thanks, and calling the hostess bade her set another cover, whilst me he invited to share his supper. And as we ate he again urged upon me the advice that I should go abroad.

"For by Heaven," he added, "Mazarin has been as a raging beast since the news was brought him yesterday of his nephew's marriage."

"How?" I cried. "He has heard already?"

"He has, indeed; and should he learn that your flesh still walks the earth, methinks it would go worse with you than it went even with Eugène de Canaples."

In answer to the questions with which I excitedly plied him, I drew from him the story of how Eugène had arrived the day before in Paris, and gone straight to the Palais Royal. M. de Montrésor had been on guard in the ante-chamber, and in virtue of an excitement noticeable in Canaples's bearing, coupled with the ill-odour wherein already he was held by Mazarin, the lieutenant's presence had been commanded in the Cardinal's closet during the interview—for his Eminence was never like to acquire fame for valour.

In his exultation at what had chanced, and at the manner in which Mazarin's Château en Espagne had been dispelled, Canaples used little caution, or even discretion, in what he said. In fact, from what Montrésor told me, I gathered that the fool's eagerness to be the first to bear the tidings to Mazarin sprang from a rash desire to gloat over the Cardinal's discomfiture. He had told his story insolently—almost derisively—and Mazarin's fury, driven beyond bounds already by what he had heard, became a very tempest of passion 'neath the lash of Canaples's impertinences. And, naturally enough, that tempest had burst upon the only head available—Eugène de Canaples's—and the Cardinal had answered his jibes with interest by calling upon Montrésor to arrest the fellow and bear him to the Bastille.

When the astonished and sobered Canaples had indignantly asked upon what charge he was being robbed of his liberty, the Cardinal had laughed at him, and answered with his never-failing axiom that "He who sings, pays."

"You sang lustily enough just now," his Eminence had added, "and you shall pay by lodging awhile in an oubliette of the Bastille, where you may lift up your voice to sing the De profundis."

"Was my name not mentioned?" I anxiously inquired when Montrésor had finished.

"Not once. You may depend that I should have remarked it. After I had taken Canaples away, the Cardinal, I am told, sat down, and, still trembling with rage, wrote a letter which he straightway dispatched to the Chevalier Armand de Canaples, at Blois.

"No doubt," I mused, "he attributes much blame to me for what has come to pass."

"Not a doubt of it. This morning he said to me that it was a pity your wings had not been clipped before you left Paris, and that his misplaced clemency had helped to bring him great misfortunes. You see, therefore, M. de Luynes, that your sojourn in France will be attended with great peril. I advise you to try Spain; 't is a martial country where a man of the sword may find honourable and even profitable employment."

His counsel I deemed sound. But how follow it? Then of a sudden I bethought me of Madame de Chevreuse's friendly letter. Doubtless she would assist me once again, and in such an extremity as this. And with the conception of the thought came the resolution to visit her on the morrow. That formed, I gave myself up to the task of drinking M. de Montrésor under the table with an abandon which had not been mine for months. In each goblet that I drained, methought I saw Yvonne's sweet face floating on the surface of the red Armagnac; it looked now sad, now reproachful, still I drank on, and in each cup I pledged her.

CHAPTER XX

OF HOW THE CHEVALIER DE CANAPLES BECAME A FRONDEUR

It wanted an hour or so to noon next day as I drove across the Pont Neuf in a closed carriage, and was borne down the Rue St. Dominique to the portals of that splendid palace, facing the Jacobins, which bears the title of the "Hôtel de Luynes," and over the portals of which is carved the escutcheon of our house.

Michelot—in obedience to the orders I had given him—got down only to be informed that Madame la Duchesse was in the country. The lackey who was summoned did not know where the lady might be found, nor when she might return to Paris. And so I was compelled to drive back almost despairingly to the Rue St. Antoine, and there lie concealed, nursing my impatience, until my aunt should return.

Daily I sent Michelot to the Hôtel de Luynes to make the same inquiry, and to return daily with the same dispiriting reply—that there was no news of Madame la Duchesse.

In this fashion some three weeks wore themselves out, during which period I lay in my concealment, a prey to weariness unutterable. I might not venture forth save at night, unless I wore a mask; and as masks were no longer to be worn without attracting notice—as during the late king's reign—I dared not indulge the practice.

Certainly my ennui was greatly relieved by the visits of Montrésor, which grew very frequent, the lad appearing to have conceived a kindness

150

for me; and during those three weeks our fellowship at nights over a bottle or two engendered naturally enough a friendship and an intimacy between us.

I had written to Andrea on the morrow of my return to Paris, to tell him how kindly Montrésor had dealt with me, and some ten days later the following letter was brought me by the lieutenant—to whom, for safety, it had been forwarded:

"MY VERY DEAR GASTON:

I have no words wherewith to express my joy at the good news you send me, which terminates the anxiety that has been mine since you left us on the disastrous morning of our nuptials.

The uncertainty touching your fate, the fear that the worst might have befallen you, and the realisation that I—for whom you have done so much—might do naught for you in your hour of need, has been the one cloud to mar the sunshine of my own bliss.

That cloud your letter has dispelled, and the knowledge of your safety renders my happiness complete.

The Chevalier maintains his unforgiving mood, as no doubt doth also my Lord Cardinal. But what to me are the frowns of either, so that my lady smile? My little Geneviève is yet somewhat vexed in spirit at all this, but I am teaching her to have faith in Time, the patron saint of all lovers who follow not the course their parents set them. And so that time may be allowed to intercede and appeal to the parent heart with the potent prayer of a daughter's absence, I shall take my lady from Chambord some three days hence. We shall travel by easy stages to Marseilles, and there take ship for Palermo.

And so, dear, trusty friend, until we meet again, fare you well and may God hold you safe from the wickedness of man, devil, and my Lord Cardinal.

For all that you have done for me, no words of mine can thank you, but should you determine to quit this France of yours, and journey to Palermo after me, you shall never want a roof to shelter you or a board to sit at, so long as roof and board are owned by him who signs himself, in love at least, your brother—

ANDREA DE MANCINI."

With a sigh I set the letter down. A sigh of love and gratitude it was; a sigh also of regret for the bright, happy boy who had been the source alike of my recent joys and sorrows, and whom methought I was not likely to see again for many a day, since the peaceful vegetation of his Sicilian home held little attraction for me, a man of action.

It was on the evening of the last Sunday in May, whilst the bell of the Jesuits, close by, was tinkling out its summons to vespers, that Montrésor burst suddenly into my room with the request that I should get my hat and cloak and go with him to pay a visit. In reply to my questions— "Monseigneur's letter to Armand de Canaples," he said, "has borne fruit already. Come with me and you shall learn how."

He led me past the Bastille and up the Rue des Tournelles to the door of an unpretentious house, upon which he knocked. We were admitted by an old woman to whom Montrésor appeared to be known, for, after exchanging a word or two with her, he himself led the way upstairs and opened the door of a room for me.

By the melancholy light of a single taper burning upon the table I beheld a fair-sized room containing a curtained bed.

My companion took up the candle, and stepping to the bedside, he drew apart the curtains.

Lying there I beheld a man whose countenance, despite its pallor and the bloody bandages about his brow, I recognised for that of the little spitfire Malpertuis.

As the light fell upon his face, the little fellow opened his eyes, and upon beholding me at his side he made a sudden movement which wrung from him a cry of pain.

"Lie still, Monsieur," said Montrésor quietly.

But for all the lieutenant's remonstrances, he struggled up into a sitting posture, requesting Montrésor to set the pillows at his back.

"Thank God you are here, M. de Luynes!" he said. "I learnt at Canaples that you were not dead."

"You have been to Canaples?"

"I was a guest of the Chevalier for twelve days. I arrived there on the day after your departure."

"You!" I ejaculated. "Pray what took you to Canaples?"

"What took me there?" he echoed, turning his feverish eyes upon me, almost with fierceness. "The same motive that led me to join hands with that ruffian St. Auban, when he spoke of waging war against Mancini; the same motive that led me to break with him when I saw through his plans, and when the abduction of Mademoiselle was on foot; the same motive that made me come to you and tell you of the proposed abduction so that you might interfere if you had the power, or cause others to do so if you had not."

I lay back in my chair and stared at him. Was this, then, another suitor of Yvonne de Canaples, and were all men mad with love of her?

Presently he continued:

"When I heard that St. Auban was in Paris, having apparently abandoned all hope in connection with Mademoiselle, I obtained a letter from M. de la Rochefoucauld—who is an intimate friend of mine—and armed with this I set out. As luck would have it I got embroiled in the streets of Blois with a couple of cardinalist gentlemen, who chose to be offended by lampoon of the Fronde that I was humming. I am not a patient man, and I am even indiscreet in moments of choler. I ended by crying, "Down with Mazarin and all his creatures," and I would of a certainty have had my throat slit, had not a slight and elegant gentleman interposed, and, exercising a wonderful influence over my assailants, extricated me from my predicament. This gentleman was the Chevalier de Canaples. He was strangely enough in a mood to be pleased by an anti-cardinalist ditty, for his rage against Andrea de Mancini—which he took no pains to conceal—had extended already to the Cardinal, and from morn till night he did little else but revile the whole Italian brood—as he chose to dub the Cardinal's family."

I recognised the old knight's weak, vacillating character in this, a creature of moods that, like the vane on a steeple, turns this way or that, as the wind blows.

"I crave your patience, M. de Luynes," he continued, "and beg of you to hear my story so that you may determine whether you will save the Canaples from the danger that threatens them. I only ask that you dispatch a reliable messenger to Blois. But hear me out first. In virtue as much of La Rochefoucauld's letters as of the sentiments which the Chevalier heard me express, I became the honoured guest at his château. Three days after my arrival I sustained a shock by the unexpected appearance at Canaples of St. Auban. The Chevalier, however, refused him admittance, and, baffled, the Marquis was forced to withdraw. But he went no farther than Blois, where he hired himself a room at the Lys de France. The Chevalier hated him as a mad dog hates water—almost as much as he hated you. He spoke often of you, and always bitterly."

Before I knew what I had said—

"And Mademoiselle?" I burst out. "Did she ever mention my name?"

Malpertuis looked up quickly at the question, and a wan smile flickered round his lips.

"Once she spoke of you to me—pityingly, as one might speak of a dead man whose life had not been good."

154

"Yes, yes," I broke in. "It matters little. Your story, M. Malpertuis."

"After I had been at the château ten days, we learnt that Eugène de Canaples had been sent to the Bastille. The news came in a letter penned by his Eminence himself—a bitter, viperish letter, with a covert threat in every line. The Chevalier's anger went white hot as he read the disappointed Cardinal's epistle. His Eminence accused Eugène of being a frondeur; M. de Canaples, whose politics had grown sadly rusted in the country, asked me the meaning of the word. I explained to him the petty squabbles between Court and Parliament, in consequence of the extortionate imposts and of Mazarin's avariciousness. I avowed myself a partisan of the Fronde, and within three days the Chevalier—who but a little time before had sought an alliance with the Cardinal's family—had become as rabid a frondeur as M. de Gondi, as fierce an anticardinalist as M. de Beaufort.

"I humoured him in his new madness, with the result that ere long from being a frondeur in heart, he thirsted to become a frondeur in deeds, and he ended by begging me to bear a letter from him to the Coadjutor of Paris, wherein he offered to place at M. de Gondi's disposal, towards the expenses of the civil war which he believed to be imminent,—as, indeed, it is,—the sum of sixty thousand livres.

"Now albeit I had gone to Canaples for purposes of my own, and not as an agent of M. le Coadjuteur's, still for many reasons I saw fit to undertake the Chevalier's commission. And so, bearing the letter in question, which was hot and unguarded, and charged with endless treasonable matter, I set out four days later for Paris, arriving here yesterday.

"I little knew that I had been followed by St. Auban. His suspicions must have been awakened, I know not how, and clearly they were confirmed when I stopped before the Coadjutor's house last night. I was about to mount the steps, when of a sudden I was seized from behind by half a dozen hands and dragged into a side street. I got free for a moment and attempted to defend myself, but besides St. Auban there were two others. They broke my sword and attempted to break my skull, in which they went perilously near succeeding, as you see. Albeit half-swooning, I had yet sufficient consciousness left to realise that my pockets were being emptied, and that at last they had torn open my doublet and withdrawn the treasonable letter from the breast of it.

"I was left bleeding in the kennel, and there I lay for nigh upon an hour until a passer-by succoured me and carried out my request to be brought hither and put to bed."

He ceased, and for some moments there was silence, broken only by the wounded man's laboured breathing, which argued that his narrative had left him fatigued. At last I sprang up.

"The Chevalier de Canaples must be warned," I exclaimed.

"'T is an ugly business," muttered Montrésor. "I'll wager a hundred that Mazarin will hang the Chevalier if he catches him just now."

"He would not dare!" cried Malpertuis.

"Not dare?" echoed the lieutenant. "The man who imprisoned the Princes of Condé and Conti, and the Duke of Beaufort, not dare hang a provincial knight with never a friend at Court! Pah, Monsieur, you do not know Cardinal Mazarin."

I realised to the full how likely Montrésor's prophecy was to be fulfilled, and before I left Malpertuis I assured him that he had not poured his story into the ears of an indifferent listener, and that I would straightway find means of communicating with Canaples.

CHAPTER XXI

OF THE BARGAIN THAT ST. AUBAN DROVE WITH MY LORD CARDINAL

From the wounded man's bedside I wended my steps back to the Rue St. Antoine, resolved to start for Blois that very night; and beside me walked Montrésor, with bent head, like a man deep in thought.

At my door I paused to take my leave of the lieutenant, for I was in haste to have my preparations made, and to be gone. But Montrésor appeared not minded to be dismissed thus easily.

"What plan have you formed?" he asked.

"The only plan there is to form—to set out for Canaples at once."

"Hum!" he grunted, and again was silent. Then, suddenly throwing back his head, "Par la mort Dieu!" he cried, "I care not what comes of it; I'll tell you what I know. Lead the way to your chamber, M. de Luynes, and delay your departure until you have heard me."

Surprised as much by his words as by the tone in which he uttered them, which was that of a man who is angry with himself, I passively did as I was bidden.

Once within my little ante-chamber, he turned the key with his own hands, and pointing to the door of my bedroom—"In there, Monsieur," quoth he, "we shall be safe from listeners."

Deeper grew my astonishment at all this mystery, as we passed into the room beyond.

"Now, M. de Luynes," he cried, flinging down his hat, "for no apparent reason I am about to commit treason; I am about to betray the hand that pays me."

"If no reason exists, why do so evil a deed?" I inquired calmly. "I have learnt during our association to wish you well, Montrésor; if by telling me that which your tongue burns to tell, you shall have cause for shame, the door is yonder. Go before harm is done, and leave me alone to fight my battle out."

He stood up, and for a moment he seemed to waver, then dismissing his doubts with an abrupt gesture, he sat down again.

"There is no wrong in what I do. Right is with you, M. de Luynes, and if I break faith with the might I serve, it is because that might is an unjust one; I do but betray the false to the true, and there can be little shame in such an act. Moreover, I have a reason—but let that be."

He was silent for a moment, then he resumed:

"Most of that which you have learnt from Malpertuis tonight, I myself could have told you. Yes; St. Auban has carried Canaples's letter to the Cardinal already. I heard from his lips today—for I was present at the interview—how the document had been wrested from Malpertuis. For your sake, so that you might learn all he knew, I sought the fellow out, and having found him in the Rue des Tournelles, I took you thither."

In a very fever of excitement I listened.

"To take up the thread of the story where Malpertuis left off, let me tell you that St. Auban sought an audience with Mazarin this morning, and by virtue of a note which he desired an usher to deliver to his Eminence, he was admitted, the first of all the clients that for hours had thronged the ante-room. As in the instance of the audience to Eugène de Canaples, so upon this occasion did it chance that the Cardinal's fears touching St. Auban's purpose had been roused, for he bade me stand behind the curtains in his cabinet.

"The Marquis spoke bluntly enough, and with rude candour he stated that since Mazarin had failed to bring the Canaples estates into his family by marriage, he came to set before his Eminence a proof so utter of Canaples's treason that it would enable him to snatch the estates by confiscation. The Cardinal may have been staggered by St. Auban's bluntness, but his avaricious instincts led him to stifle his feelings and bid the Marquis to set this proof before him. But St. Auban had a bargain to drive—a preposterous one methought. He demanded that in return for his delivering into the hands of Mazarin the person of Armand de Canaples together with an incontestable proof that the Chevalier was in league with the frondeurs, and had offered to place a large sum of money at their disposal, he was to receive as recompense the demesne of Canaples on the outskirts of Blois, together with one third of the confiscated estates. At first Mazarin gasped at his audacity, then laughed at him, whereupon St. Auban politely craved his Eminence's permission to withdraw. This the Cardinal, however, refused him, and bidding him remain, he sought to bargain with him. But the Marquis replied that he was unversed in the ways of trade and barter, and that he had no mind to enter into them. From bargaining the Cardinal passed on to threatening and from threatening to whining, and so on until the end—St. Auban preserving a firm demeanour—the comedy was played out and Mazarin fell in with his proposal and his terms.

"Mille diables!" I cried. "And has St. Auban set out?"

"He starts tomorrow, and I go with him. When finally the Cardinal had consented, the Marquis demanded and obtained from him a promise in writing, signed and sealed by Mazarin, that he should receive a third of the Canaples estates and the demesne on the outskirts of Blois, in exchange for the body of Armand de Canaples, dead or alive, and a proof of treason sufficient to warrant his arrest and the confiscation of his estates. Next, seeing in what regard the Seigneur is held by the people of Blois, and fearing that his arrest might be opposed by many of his adherents, the Marquis has demanded a troop of twenty men. This Mazarin has also granted him, entrusting the command of the troop to me, under St. Auban. Further, the Marquis has stipulated that the greatest secrecy is to be observed, and has expressed his purpose of going upon this enterprise disguised and masked, for—as he rightly opines—when months hence he enters into possession of the demesne of Canaples in the character of purchaser, did the Blaisois recognise in him the man who sold the Chevalier, his life would stand in hourly peril."

I heard him through patiently enough; yet when he stopped, my pent-up feelings burst all bonds, and I resolved there and then to go in quest of that Judas, St. Auban, and make an end of his plotting, for all time. But Montrésor restrained me, showing me how futile such a course must prove, and how I risked losing all chance of aiding those at Canaples.

He was right. First I must warn the Chevalier—afterwards I would deal with St. Auban.

Someone knocked at that moment, and with the entrance of Michelot, my talk with Montrésor came perforce to an end. For Michelot brought me the news that for days I had been awaiting; Madame de Chevreuse had returned to Paris at last.

But for Montrésor's remonstrances it is likely that I should have set out forthwith to wait upon her. I permitted myself, however, to be persuaded that the lateness of the hour would render my visit unwelcome, and so I determined in the end—albeit grudgingly—to put off my departure for Blois until the morrow.

Noon had but struck from Nôtre Dame, next day, as I mounted the steps of the Hôtel de Luynes. My swagger, and that brave suit of pearl grey velvet with its silver lace, bore me unchallenged past the gorgeous suisse, who stood, majestic, in the doorway.

But, for the first mincing lackey I chanced upon, more was needed to gain me an audience. And so, as I did not choose to speak my name, I drew a ring from my finger and bade him bear it to the Duchesse.

He obeyed me in this, and presently returning, he bowed low and begged of me to follow him, for, as I had thought, albeit Madame de Chevreuse might not know to whom that ring belonged, yet the arms of Luynes carved upon the stone had sufficed to ensure an interview.

I was ushered into a pretty boudoir, hung in blue and gold, which overlooked the garden, and wherein, reclining upon a couch, with a book of Bois Robert's verses in her white and slender hand, I found my beautiful aunt.

Of this famous lady, who was the cherished friend and more than sister of Anne of Austria, much has been written; much that is good, and more—far more—that is ill, for those who have a queen for friend shall never lack for enemies. But those who have praised and those who have censured have at least been at one touching her marvellous beauty. At the time whereof I write it is not possible that she could be less than forty-six, and yet her figure was slender and shapely and still endowed with the grace of girlhood; her face delicate of tint, and little marked by time—or even by the sufferings to which, in the late king's reign, Cardinal de Richelieu had subjected her; her eyes were blue and peaceful as a summer sky; her hair was the colour of ripe corn. He would be a hardy guesser who set her age at so much as thirty.

My appearance she greeted by letting fall her book, and lifting up her hands—the loveliest in France—she uttered a little cry of surprise.

"Is it really you, Gaston?" she asked.

Albeit it was growing wearisome to be thus greeted by all to whom I showed myself, yet I studied courtesy in my reply, and then, 'neath the suasion of her kindliness, I related all that had befallen me since first I had journeyed to Blois, in Andrea de Mancini's company, withholding, however, all allusions to my feelings towards Yvonne. Why betray them when they were doomed to be stifled in the breast that begat them? But Madame de Chevreuse had not been born a woman and lived six and forty years to no purpose.

"And this maid with as many suitors as Penelope, is she very beautiful?" she inquired slyly.

"France does not hold her equal," I answered, falling like a simpleton into the trap she had set me.

"This to me?" quoth she archly. "Fi donc, Gaston! Your evil ways have taught you as little gallantry as dissimulation." And her merry ripple of laughter showed me how in six words I had betrayed that which I had been at such pains to hide.

But before I could, by protestations, plunge deeper than I stood already, the Duchesse turned the conversation adroitly to the matter of that letter of hers, wherein she had bidden me wait upon her.

A cousin of mine—one Marion de Luynes, who, like myself, had, through the evil of his ways, become an outcast from his family—was lately dead. Unlike me, however, he was no adventurous soldier of fortune, but a man of peace, with an estate in Provence that had a rent-roll of five thousand livres a year. On his death-bed he had cast about him for an heir, unwilling that his estate should swell the fortunes of the family that in life had disowned him. Into his ear some kindly angel had whispered my name, and the memory that I shared with him the frowns of our house, and that my plight must be passing pitiful, had set up a bond of sympathy between us, which had led him to will his lands to me. Of Madame de Chevreuse—who clearly was the patron saint of those of her first husband's nephews who chanced to tread ungodly ways—my cousin Marion had besought that she should see to the fulfilment of his last wishes.

My brain reeled beneath the first shock of that unlooked-for news. Already I saw myself transformed from a needy adventurer into a gentleman of fortune, and methought my road to Yvonne lay open, all obstacles removed. But swiftly there followed the thought of my own position, and truly it seemed that a cruel irony lay in the manner wherein things had fallen out, since did I declare myself to be alive and claim the Provence estates, the Cardinal's claws would be quick to seize me.

Thus much I told Madame de Chevreuse, but her answer cheered me, and said much for my late cousin's prudence.

"Nay," she cried. "Marion was ever shrewd. Knowing that men who live by the sword, as you have lived, are often wont to die by the sword,—

162

and that suddenly at times,—he has made provision that in the event of your being dead his estates shall come to me, who have been the most indulgent of his relatives. This, my dear Gaston, has already taken place, for we believed you dead; and therein fortune has been kind to you, for now, while receiving the revenues of your lands—which the world will look upon as mine—I shall contrive that they reach you wherever you may be, until such a time as you may elect to come to life again."

Now but for the respect in which I held her, I could have taken the pretty Duchesse in my arms and kissed her.

Restraining myself, however, I contented myself by kissing her hand, and told her of the journey I was going, then craved another boon of her. No matter what the issue of that journey, and whether I went alone or accompanied, I was determined to quit France and repair to Spain. There I would abide until the Parliament, the Court, or the knife of some chance assassin, or even Nature herself should strip Mazarin of his power.

Now, at the Court of Spain it was well known that my aunt's influence was vast, and so, the boon I craved was that she should aid me to a position in the Spanish service that would allow me during my exile to find occupation and perchance renown. To this my aunt most graciously acceded, and when at length I took my leave—with such gratitude in my heart that what words I could think of seemed but clumsily to express it—I bore in the breast of my doublet a letter to Don Juan de Cordova—a noble of great prominence at the Spanish Court—and in the pocket of my haut-de-chausses a rouleau of two hundred gold pistoles, as welcome as they were heavy.

CHAPTER XXII

OF MY SECOND JOURNEY TO CANAPLES

An hour after I had quitted the Hôtel de Luynes, Michelot and I left Paris by the barrier St. Michel and took the Orleans road. How different it looked in the bright June sunshine, to the picture which it had presented to our eyes on that February evening, four months ago, when last we had set out upon that same journey!

Not only in nature had a change been wrought, but in my very self. My journey then had been aimless, and I had scarcely known whither I was bound nor had I fostered any great concern thereon. Now I rode in hot haste with a determined purpose, a man of altered fortunes and altered character.

Into Choisy we clattered at a brisk pace, but at the sight of the inn of the Connétable such memories surged up that I was forced to draw rein and call for a cup of Anjou, which I drank in the saddle. Thereafter we rode without interruption through Longjumeau, Arpajon, and Etrechy, and so well did we use our horses that as night fell we reached Étampes.

From inquiries that Michelot had made on the road, we learned that no troop such as that which rode with St. Auban had lately passed that way, so that 't was clear we were in front of them.

But scarce had we finished supper in the little room which I had hired at the Gros Paon, when, from below, a stamping of hoofs, the jangle of arms, and the shouts of many men told me that we were overtaken.

Clearly I did not burn with a desire to linger, but rather it seemed to me that although night had closed in, black and moonless, we must set out again, and push on to Monnerville, albeit our beasts were worn and the distance a good three leagues.

With due precaution we effected our departure, and thereafter had a spur been needed to speed us on our way that spur we had in the knowledge that St. Auban came close upon our heels. At Monnerville we slept, and next morning we were early afoot; by four o'clock in the afternoon we had reached Orleans, whence—with fresh horses—we pursued our journey as far as Meung, where we lay that night.

There we were joined by a sturdy rascal whom Michelot enlisted into my service, seeing that not only did my means allow, but the enterprise upon which I went might perchance demand another body servant. This recruit was a swart, powerfully built man of about my own age; trusty, and a lover of hard knocks, as Michelot—who had long counted him among his friends—assured me. He owned the euphonious name of Abdon.

I spent twenty pistoles in suitable raiment and a horse for him, and as we left Meung next day the knave cut a brave enough figure that added not a little to my importance to have at my heels.

This, however, so retarded our departure, that night had fallen by the time we reached Blois. Still our journey had been a passing swift one. We had left Paris on a Monday, the fourth of June—I have good cause to remember, since on that day I entered both upon my thirty-second year and my altered fortunes; on the evening of Wednesday we reached Blois, having covered a distance of forty-three leagues in less than three days.

Bidding Michelot carry my valise to the hostelry of the Vigne d'Or, and there await my coming, I called to Abdon to attend me, and rode on, jaded and travel-stained though I was, to Canaples, realising fully that there was no time to lose.

Old Guilbert, who came in answer to my knock at the door of the château, looked askance when he beheld me, and when I bade him carry my compliments to the Chevalier, with the message that I desired immediate speech of him on a matter of the gravest moment, he shook his grey head and protested that it would be futile to obey me. Yet, in the end, when I had insisted, he went upon my errand, but only to return with a disturbed countenance, to tell me that the Chevalier refused to see me.

"But I must speak to him, Guilbert," I exclaimed, setting foot upon the top step. "I have travelled expressly from Paris."

The man stood firm and again shook his head.

"I beseech you not to insist, Monsieur. M. le Chevalier has sworn to dismiss me if I permit you to set foot within the château."

"Mille diables! This is madness! I seek to serve him," I cried, my temper rising fast. "At least, Guilbert, will you tell Mademoiselle that I am here, and that I—"

"I may carry no more messages for you, Monsieur," he broke in. "Listen! There is M. le Chevalier."

In reality I could hear the old knight's voice, loud and shrill with anger, and a moment later Louis, his intendant, came across the hall.

"Guilbert," he commanded harshly, "close the door. The night air is keen."

My cheeks aflame with anger, I still made one last attempt to gain an audience.

"Master Louis," I exclaimed, "will you do me the favour to tell M. de Canaples—"

"You are wasting time, Monsieur," he interrupted. "M. de Canaples will not see you. He bids you close the door, Guilbert."

"Pardieu! he shall see me!"

"The door, Guilbert!"

I took a step forward, but before I could gain the threshold, the door was slammed in my face, and as I stood there, quivering with anger and disappointment, I heard the bolts being shot within.

I turned with an oath.

"Come, Abdon," I growled, as I climbed once more into the saddle, "let us leave the fool to the fate he has chosen."

166

CHAPTER XXIII

OF HOW ST. AUBAN CAME TO BLOIS

In silence we rode back to Blois. Not that I lacked matter for conversation. Anger and chagrin at the thought that I had come upon this journey to earn naught but an insult and to have a door slammed in my face made my gorge rise until it went near to choking me. I burned to revile Canaples aloud, but Abdon's was not the ear into which I might pour the hot words that welled up to my lips.

Yet if silent, the curses that I heaped upon the Chevalier's crassness were none the less fervent, and to myself I thought with grim relish of how soon and how dearly he would pay for the affront he had put upon me.

That satisfaction, however, endured not long; for presently I bethought me of how heavily the punishment would fall upon Yvonne—and yet, of how she would be left to the mercy of St. Auban, whose warrant from Mazarin would invest with almost any and every power at Canaples.

I ground my teeth at the sudden thought, and for a moment I was on the point of going back and forcing my way into the château at the sword point if necessary, to warn and save the Chevalier in spite of himself and unthanked.

It was not in such a fashion that I had thought to see my mission to Canaples accomplished; I had dreamt of gratitude, and gratitude unbars the door to much. Nevertheless, whether or not I earned it, I must return, and succeed where for want of insistence I had failed awhile ago.

Of a certainty I should have acted thus, but that at the very moment upon which I formed the resolution Abdon drew my attention to a dark shadow by the roadside not twenty paces in front of us. This proved to be the motionless figure of a horseman.

As soon as I was assured of it, I reined in my horse, and taking a pistol from the holster, I levelled it at the shadow, accompanying the act by a sonorous—

"Who goes there?"

The shadow stirred, and Michelot's voice answered me:

'T is I, Monsieur. They have arrived. I came to warn you."

"Who has arrived?" I shouted.

"The soldiers. They are lodged at the Lys de France."

An oath was the only comment I made as I turned the news over in my mind. I must return to Canaples.

Then another thought occurred to me. The Chevalier was capable of going to extremes to keep me from entering his house; he might for instance greet me with a blunderbuss. It was not the fear of that that deterred me, but the fear that did a charge of lead get mixed with my poor brains before I had said what I went to say, matters would be no better, and there would be one poor knave the less to adorn the world.

"What shall we do, Michelot?" I groaned, appealing in my despair to my henchman.

"Might it not be well to seek speech with M. de Montrésor?" quoth he.

I shrugged my shoulders. Nevertheless, after a moment's deliberation I determined to make the attempt; if I succeeded something might come of it.

And so I pushed on to Blois with my knaves close at my heels.

Up the Rue Vieille we proceeded with caution, for the hostelry of the Vigne d'Or, where Michelot had hired me a room, fortunately overlooking the street, fronted the Lys de France, where St. Auban and his men were housed.

168

I gained that room of mine without mishap, and my first action was to deal summarily with a fat and well-roasted capon which the landlord set before me—for an empty stomach is a poor comrade in a desperate situation. That meal, washed down with the best part of a bottle of red Anjou, did much to restore me alike in body and in mind.

From my open window I gazed across the street at the Lys de France. The door of the common-room, opening upon the street, was set wide, and across the threshold came a flood of light in which there flitted the black figures of maybe a dozen amazed rustics, drawn thither for all the world as bats are drawn to a glare.

And there they hovered with open mouths and stupid eyes, hearkening to the din of voices that floated out on the tranquil air, the snatches of ribald songs, the raucous bursts of laughter, the clink of glasses, the clank of steel, the rattle of dice, and the strange soldier oaths that fell with every throw, and which to them must have sounded almost as words of some foreign tongue.

Whilst I stood by my window, the landlord entered my room, and coming up to me—

"Thank Heaven they are not housed at the Vigne d'Or," he said. "It will take Maître Bernard a week to rid his house of the stench of leather. They are part of a stray company that is on its way to fight the Spaniards," he informed me. "But methinks they will be forced to spend two or three days at Blois; their horses are sadly jaded and will need that rest before they can take the road again, thanks to the pace at which their boy of an officer must have led them. There is a gentleman with them who wears a mask. 'T is whispered that he is a prince of the blood who has made a vow not to uncover his face until this war be ended, in expiation of some sin committed in mad Paris."

I heard him in silence, and when he had done I thanked him for his information. So! This was the story that the crafty St. Auban had spread abroad to lull suspicion touching the real nature of their presence until their horses should be fit to undertake the return journey to Paris, or until he should have secured the person of M. de Canaples.

Towards eleven o'clock, as the lights in the hostelry opposite were burning low, I descended, and made my way out into the now deserted street. The troopers had apparently seen fit—or else been ordered—to seek their beds, for the place had grown silent, and a servant was in the act of making fast the door for the night. The porte-cochère was half closed, and a man carrying a lantern was making fast the bolt, whistling aimlessly to himself. Through the half of the door that was yet open, I beheld a window from which the light fell upon a distant corner of the courtyard.

I drew near the fellow with the lantern, in whom I recognised René, the hostler, and as I approached he flashed the light upon my face; then with a gasp—"M. de Luynes," he exclaimed, remembering me from the time when I had lodged at the Lys de France, three months ago.

"Sh!" I whispered, pressing a louis d'or into his hand. "Whose window is that, René?" And I pointed towards the light.

"That," he replied, "is the room of the lieutenant and the gentleman in the mask."

"I must take a look at them, René, and whilst I am looking I shall search my pocket for another louis. Now let me in."

"I dare not, Monsieur. Maître Bernard may call me, and if the doors are not closed—"

"Dame!" I broke in. "I shall stay but a moment."

"But—"

"And you will have easily earned a louis d'or. If Bernard calls you—peste, tell him that you have let fall something, and that you are seeking it. There, let me pass."

1 got past him at last, and made my way swiftly towards the other end of the quadrangle.

As I approached, the sound of voices smote my ear, for the lighted window stood open. I stopped within half a dozen paces of it, and climbed on to the step of a coach that stood there. Thence I could look straight into the room, whilst the darkness hid me from the eyes of those I watched.

Three men there were; Montrésor, the sergeant of his troop, and a tall man dressed in black, and wearing a black silk mask. This I concluded to be St. Auban, despite the profusion of fair locks that fell upon his shoulders, concealing—I rightly guessed—his natural hair, which was as black as my own. It was a cunning addition to his disguise, and one well calculated to lead people on to the wrong scent hereafter.

Presently, as I watched them, St. Auban spoke, and his voice was that of a man whose gums are toothless, or else whose nether lip is drawn in over his teeth whilst he speaks. Here again the dissimulation was as effective as it was simple.

"So; that is concluded," were the words that reached me. "Tomorrow we will install our men at the château, for while we remain here it is preposterous to lodge them at an inn. On the following day I hope that we may be able to set out again."

"If we could obtain fresh horses—" began the sergeant, when he of the mask interrupted him.

"Sangdieu! Think you my purse is bottomless? We return as we came, with the Cardinal's horses. What signify a day or two, after all? Come—call the landlord to light me to my room."

I had heard enough. But more than that, whilst I listened, an idea had of a sudden sprung up in my mind which did away with the necessity of gaining speech with Montresor—a contingency, moreover, that now presented insuperable difficulties.

So I got down softly from my perch and made my way out of the yard, and, after fulfilling my part of the bargain with René, across to the Vigne d'Or and to my room, there to sit and mature the plan that of a sudden I had conceived.

CHAPTER XXIV

OF THE PASSING OF ST. AUBAN

Dame! What an ado there was next day in Blois, when the news came that the troopers had installed themselves at the Château de Canaples and that the Chevalier had been arrested for treason by order of the Lord Cardinal, and that he would be taken to Paris, and—probably—the scaffold.

Men gathered in little knots at street corners, and with sullen brows and threatening gestures they talked of the affair; and the more they talked, the more clouded grew their looks, and more than one anti-cardinalist pasquinade was heard in Blois that day.

Given a leader those men would have laid hands upon pikes and muskets, and gone to the Chevalier's rescue. As I observed them, the thought did cross my mind that I might contrive a pretty fight in the rose garden of Canaples were I so inclined. And so inclined I should, indeed, have been but for the plan that had come to me like an inspiration from above, and which methought would prove safer in the end.

To carry out this plan of mine, I quitted Blois at nightfall, with my two knaves, having paid my reckoning at the Lys de France, and given out that we were journeying to Tours. We followed the road that leads to Canaples, until we reached the first trees bordering the park. There I dismounted, and, leaving Abdon to guard the horses, I made my way on foot, accompanied by Michelot, towards the garden.

We gained this, and were on the point of quitting the shadow of the trees, when of a sudden, by the light of the crescent moon, I beheld a man walking in one of the alleys, not a hundred paces from where we stood. I had but time to seize Michelot by the collar of his pourpoint and draw him towards me. But as he trod precipitately backwards a twig snapped 'neath his foot with a report that in the surrounding stillness was like a pistol shot.

I caught my breath as he who walked in the garden stood still, his face, wrapped in the shadows of his hat, turned towards us.

"Who goes there?" he shouted. Then getting no reply he came resolutely forward, whilst I drew a pistol wherewith to welcome him did he come too near.

On he came, and already I had brought my pistol to a level with his head, when fortunately he repeated his question, "Who goes there?"— and this time I recognised the voice of Montrésor, the very man I could then most wish to meet.

"Hist! Montrésor!" I called softly. "'T is I—Luynes."

"So!" he exclaimed, coming close up to me. "You have reached Canaples at last!"

"At last?" I echoed.

"Whom have you there?" he inquired abruptly.

"Only Michelot."

"Bid him fall behind a little."

When Michelot had complied with this request, "You see, M. de Luynes," quoth the officer, "that you have arrived too late."

There was a certain coldness in his tone that made me seek by my reply to sound him.

"Indeed, I trust not, my friend. With your assistance I hope to get M. de Canaples from the clutches of St. Auban."

He shook his head.

"It is impossible that I should help you," he replied with increasing coldness. "Already once for your sake have I broken faith to those who pay me, by setting you in a position to forestall St. Auban and get M. de Canaples away before his arrival. Unfortunately, you have dallied on the road, M. de Luynes, and Canaples is already a prisoner—a doomed one, I fear."

"Is that your last word, Montrésor?" I inquired sadly.

"I am sorry," he answered in softened tones, "but you must see that I cannot do otherwise. I warned you; more you cannot expect of me."

I sighed, and stood musing for an instant. Then—"You are right, Montrésor. Nevertheless, I am still grateful to you for the warning you gave me in Paris. God pity and help Canaples! Adieu, Montrésor. I do not think that you will see me again."

He took my hand, but as he did so he pushed me back into the shadow from which I had stepped to proffer it him.

"Peste!" he ejaculated. "The moon was full upon your face, and did St. Auban chance to look out, he must have seen you."

I followed the indication of his thumb, and noted the lighted window to which he pointed. A moment later he was gone, and as I joined Michelot, I chuckled softly to myself.

For two hours and more I sat in the shrubbery, conversing in whispers with Michelot, and watching the lights in the château die out one by one, until St. Auban's window, which opened on to the terrace balcony, was the only one that was not wrapt in darkness.

I waited a little while longer, then rising I cautiously made a tour of inspection. Peace reigned everywhere, and the only sign of life was the sentry, who with musket on shoulder paced in front of the main entrance, a silent testimony of St. Auban's mistrust of the Blaisois and of his fears of a possible surprise.

Satisfied that everyone slept I retraced my steps to the shrubbery where Michelot awaited me, watching the square of light, and after exchanging word with him, I again stepped forth.

When I was half way across the intervening space of garden, treading with infinite precaution, a dark shadow obscured the window, which a

174

second later was thrown open. Crouching hastily behind a boxwood hedge, I watched St. Auban—for I guessed that he it was—as he leaned out and gazed skywards.

For a little while he remained there, then he withdrew, leaving the casement open, and presently I caught the grating of a chair on the parquet floor within. If ever the gods favoured mortal, they favoured me at that moment.

Stealthily as a cat I sprang towards the terrace, the steps to which I climbed on hands and knees. Stooping, I sped silently across it until I had gained the flower-bed immediately below the window that had drawn me to it. Crouching there—for did I stand upright my chin would be on a level with the sill—I paused to listen for some moments. The only sound I caught was a rustle, as of paper. Emboldened, I took a deep breath, and standing up I gazed straight into the chamber.

By the light of four tapers in heavy silver sconces, I beheld St. Auban seated at a table littered with parchments, over which he was intently poring. His back was towards me, and his long black hair hung straight upon his shoulders. On the table, amid the papers, lay his golden wig and black mask, and on the floor in the centre of the room, his back and breast of blackened steel and his sword.

It needed but little shrewdness to guess those parchments before him to be legal documents touching the Canaples estates, and his occupation that of casting up exactly what profit he would reap from his infamous work of betrayal.

So intent was the hound upon his calculations that my cautious movements passed unheeded by him as I got astride of the window ledge. It was only when I swung my right leg into the room that he turned his head, but before his eyes reached me I was standing upright and motionless within the chamber.

I have seen fear of many sorts writ large upon the faces of men of many conditions—from the awe that blanches the cheek of the boy soldier when first he hears the cannon thundering to the terror that glazes the eye of the vanquished swordsman who at every moment expects the deadly point in his heart. But never had I gazed upon a countenance filled with such abject ghastly terror as that which came over St. Auban's when his eyes met mine that night.

He sprang up with an inarticulate cry that sank into something that I can but liken to the rattle which issues from the throat of expiring men. For a second he stood where he had risen, then terror loosened his knees, and he sank back into his chair. His mouth fell open, and the trembling lips were drawn down at the corners like those of a sobbing child; his cheeks turned whiter than the lawn collar at his throat, and his eyes, wide open in a horrid stare, were fixed on mine and, powerless to avert them, he met my gaze—cold, stern, and implacable.

For a moment we remained thus, and I marvelled greatly to see a man whose heart, if full of evil, I had yet deemed stout enough, stricken by fear into so parlous and pitiful a condition.

Then I had the explanation of it as he lifted his right hand and made the sign of the cross, first upon himself, then in the air, whilst his lips moved, and I guessed that to himself he was muttering some prayer of exorcising purport. There was the solution of the terror—sweat that stood out in beads upon his brow—he had deemed me a spectre; the spectre of a man he believed to have foully done to death on a spot across the Loire visible from the window at my back.

At last he sufficiently mastered himself to break the awful silence.

"What do you want?" he whispered; then, his voice gaining power as he used it—"Speak," he commanded. "Man or devil, speak!"

I laughed for answer, harshly, mockingly; for never had I known a fiercer, crueller mood. At the sound of that laugh, satanical though may have been its ring, he sprang up again, and unsheathing a dagger he took a step towards me.

"We shall see of what you are made," he cried. "If you blast me in the act, I'll strike you!"

I laughed again, and raising my arm I gave him the nozzle of a pistol to contemplate.

"Stand where you are, St. Auban, or, by the God above us, I'll send your ghost a-wandering," quoth I coolly.

My voice, which I take it had nothing ghostly in it, and still more the levelled pistol, which of all implements is the most unghostly, dispelled his dread. The colour crept slowly back to his cheeks, and his mouth closed with a snap of determination.

"Is it, indeed, you, master meddler?" he said. "Peste! I thought you dead these three months."

"And you are overcome with joy to find that you were in error, eh, Marquis? We Luynes die hard."

"It seems so, indeed," he answered with a cool effrontery past crediting in one who but a moment ago had looked so pitiful. "What do you seek at Canaples?"

"Many things, Marquis. You among others."

"You have come to murder me," he cried, and again alarm overspread his countenance.

"Hoity, toity, Marquis! We do not all follow the same trade. Who talks of murder? Faugh!"

Again he took a step towards me, but again the nozzle of my pistol drove him back. To have pistoled him there and then as he deserved would have brought the household about my ears, and that would have defeated my object. To have fallen upon him and slain him with silent steel would have equally embarrassed me, as you shall understand anon.

"You and I had a rendezvous at St. Sulpice des Reaux," I said calmly, "to which you came with a band of hired assassins. For this you deserve to be shot like the dog you are. But I have it in my heart to be generous to you," I added in a tone of irony. "Come, take up your sword."

"To what purpose?"

"Do you question me? Take up your sword, man, and do my bidding; thus shall you have a slender chance of life. Refuse and I pistol you without compunction. So now put on that wig and mask."

When he obeyed me in this—"Now listen, St. Auban," I said. "You and I are going together to that willow copse whither three months ago you lured Yvonne de Canaples for the purpose of abducting her. On that spot you and I shall presently face each other sword in hand, with none other to witness our meeting save God, in whose hands the issue lies. That is your chance; at the first sign that you meditate playing me any tricks, that chance is lost to you." And I tapped my pistol significantly. "Now climb out through that window."

When he had done so, I bade him stand six paces away whilst I followed, and to discourage any foolish indiscretion on his part I again showed him my pistol.

He answered me with an impatient gesture, and by the light that fell on his face I saw him sneer.

"Come on, you fool," he snarled, "and have done threatening. I'll talk to you in the copse. And tread softly lest you arouse the sentry on the other side."

Rejoiced to see the man so wide awake in him, I followed him closely across the terrace, and through the rose garden to the bank of the river. This we followed until we came at last to the belt of willows, where, having found a suitable patch of even and springy turf, I drew my sword and invited him to make ready.

"Will you not strip?" he inquired sullenly.

"I do not think so," I answered. "The night air is sharp. Nevertheless, do you make ready as best you deem fit, and that speedily, Monsieur."

With an exclamation of contempt, he divested himself of his wig, mask, and doublet, then drawing his sword, he came forward, and announced himself at my disposal.

As well you may conceive, we wasted no time in compliments, but straightway went to work, and that with a zest that drew sparks from our rapiers at the first contact.

The Marquis attacked me furiously, and therein lay his only chance; for a fierce, rude sword-play that is easily dealt with in broad daylight is vastly discomposing in such pale moonshine as lighted us. I defended myself warily, for of a sudden I had grown conscious of the danger that I ran did he once by luck or strength get past my guard with that point of his which in the spare light I could not follow closely enough to feel secure.

'Neath the fury of his onslaught I was compelled to break ground more than once, and each time he was so swift to follow up his advantage that I had ne'er a chance to retaliate.

Still fear or doubt of the issue I had none. I needed but to wait until the Marquis's fury was spent by want of breath, to make an end of it. And presently that which I waited for came about. His attack began to lag in vigour, and the pressure of his blade to need less resistance, whilst his breathing grew noisy as that of a broken-winded horse. Then with the rage of a gambler who loses at every throw, he cursed and reviled me with every thrust or lunge that I turned aside.

My turn was come; yet I held back, and let him spend his strength to the utmost drop, whilst with my elbow close against my side and by an easy play of wrist, I diverted each murderous stroke of his point that came again and again for my heart.

When at last he had wasted in blasphemies what little breath his wild exertions had left him, I let him feel on his blade the twist that heralded my first riposte. He caught the thrust, and retreated a step, his blasphemous tongue silenced, and his livid face bathed in perspiration.

Cruelly I toyed with him then, and with every disengagement I made him realise that he was mastered, and that if I withheld the coup de grâce it was but to prolong his agony. And to add to the bitterness of that agony of his, I derided him whilst I fenced; with a recitation of his many

179

sins I mocked him, showing him how ripe he was for hell, and asking him how it felt to die unshriven with such a load upon his soul.

Goaded to rage by my bitter words, he grit his teeth, and gathered what rags of strength were left him for a final effort, And before I knew what he was about, he had dropped on to his left knee, and with his body thrown forward and supported within a foot of the ground by his left arm, he came, like a snake, under my guard with his point directed upwards.

So swift had been this movement and so unlooked-for, that had I not sprung backwards in the very nick of time, this narrative of mine had ne'er been written. With a jeering laugh I knocked aside his sword, but even as I disengaged, to thrust at him, he knelt up and caught my blade in his left hand, and for all that it ate its way through the flesh to the very bones of his fingers, he clung to it with that fierce strength and blind courage that is born of despair.

Then raising himself on his knees again, he struck at me wildly. I swung aside, and as his sword, missing its goal, shot past me, I caught his wrist in a grip from which I contemptuously invited him to free himself. With that began a fierce tugging and panting on both sides, which, however, was of short duration, for presently, my blade, having severed the last sinew of his fingers, was set free. Simultaneously I let go his wrist, pushing his arm from me so violently that in his exhausted condition it caused him to fall over on his side.

In an instant, however, he was up and at me again. Again our swords clashed—but once only. It was time to finish. With a vigorous disengagement I got past his feeble guard and sent my blade into him full in the middle of his chest and out again at his back until a foot or so of glittering steel protruded.

A shudder ran through him, and his mouth worked oddly, whilst spasmodically he still sought, without avail, to raise his sword; then as I recovered my blade, a half-stifled cry broke from his lips, and throwing up his arms, he staggered and fell in a heap.

As I turned him over to see if he were dead, his eyes met mine, and were full of piteous entreaty; his lips moved, and presently I caught the words:

"I am sped, Luynes." Then struggling up, and in a louder voice: "A priest!" he gasped. "Get me a priest, Luynes. Jesu! Have mer—"

A rush of blood choked him and cut short his utterance. He writhed and twitched for a moment, then his chin sank forward and he fell back, death starkening his limbs and glazing the eyes which stared hideously upwards at the cold, pitiless moon.

Such was the passing of the Marquis César de St. Auban.

CHAPTER XXV

PLAY-ACTING

For a little while I stood gazing down at my work, my mind full of the unsolvable mysteries of life and death; then I bethought me that time stood not still for me, and that something yet remained to be accomplished ere my evening's task were done.

And forthwith I made shift to do a thing at the memory of which my blood is chilled and my soul is filled with loathing even now—albeit the gulf of many years separates me from that June night at Canaples.

To pass succinctly o'er an episode on which I have scant heart to tarry, suffice it you to know that using my sash as a rope I bound a heavy stone to St. Auban's ankle; then lifting the body in my arms, I half dragged, half bore it across the little stretch of intervening sward to the water's edge, and flung it in.

As I write I have the hideous picture in my mind, and again I can see St. Auban's ghastly face grinning up at me through the moonlit waters, until at last it was mercifully swallowed up in their black depths, and naught but a circling wavelet that spread swiftly across the stream was left to tell of what had chanced.

I dare not dwell upon the feelings that assailed me as I stooped to rinse the blood from my hands, nor yet of the feverish haste wherewith I tore my blood-stained doublet from my back, and hurled it wide into the stream. For all my callousness I was sick and unmanned by that which had befallen.

No time, however, did I waste in mawkish sentiment, but setting my teeth hard, I turned away from the river, and back to the trampled ground of our recent conflict. There, with no other witness save the moon, I clad myself in the Marquis's doublet of black velvet; I set his mask of silk upon my face, his golden wig upon my head, and over that his sable hat with its drooping feather. Next I buckled on his sword belt, wherefrom hung his rapier that I had sheathed.

In Blois that day I had taken the precaution—knowing the errand upon which I came—to procure myself haut-de-chausses of black velvet, and black leather boots with gilt spurs that closely resembled those which St. Auban had worn in life.

Now, as I have already written, St. Auban and I were of much the same build and stature, and so methought with confidence that he would have shrewd eyes, indeed, who could infer from my appearance that I was other than the same masked gentleman who had that very day ridden into Canaples at the head of a troop of his Eminence's guards.

I made my way swiftly back along the path that St. Auban and I had together trodden but a little while ago, and past the château until I came to the shrubbery where Michelot—faithful to the orders I had given him—awaited my return. From his concealment he had seen me leave the château with the Marquis, and as I suddenly loomed up before him now, he took me for the man whose clothes I wore, and naturally enough assumed that ill had befallen Gaston de Luynes. Of a certainty I had been pistolled by him had I not spoken in time. I lingered but to give him certain necessary orders; then, whilst he went off to join Abdon and see to their fulfilment, I made my way stealthily, with eyes keeping watch around me, across the terrace, and through the window into the room that St. Auban had left to follow me to his death.

The tapers still burned, and in all respects the chamber was as it had been; the back and breast pieces still lay upon the floor, and on the table the littered documents. The door I ascertained had been locked on the inside, a precaution which St. Auban had no doubt taken so that none might spy upon the work that busied him.

I closed and made fast the window, then I bethought me that, being in ignorance of the whereabouts of St. Auban's bed-chamber, I must perforce spend the night as best I could within that very room.

And so I sat me down and pondered deeply o'er the work that was to come, the part I was about to play, and the details of its playing. In this manner did I while away perchance an hour; through the next one I must have slept, for I awakened with a start to find three tapers spent and the last one spluttering, and in the sky the streaks that heralded the summer dawn.

Again I fell to thinking; again I slept, and woke again to find the night gone and the sunlight on my face. Someone knocked at the door, and that knocking vibrated through my brain and set me wide-awake, indeed. It was as the signal to uplift the curtain and let my play-acting commence.

Hastily I rose and shot a glance at the mirror to see that my wig hung straight and that my mask was rightly adjusted. I started at my own reflection, for methought that from the glass 't was St. Auban who looked at me, as I had seen him look the night before when he had donned those things at my command.

"Holà there, within!" came Montrésor's voice. "Monsieur le Capitaine!" A fresh shower of blows descended on the oak panels.

I yawned with prodigious sonority, and overturned a chair with my foot. Then bracing myself for the ordeal, through which I looked to what scant information I possessed and my own mother wit, to bear me successfully, I strode across to admit my visitor.

Muffling my voice, as I had heard St. Auban do at the inn, by drawing my nether lip over my teeth—

"Pardieu!" quoth I, as I opened the door, "it seems, Lieutenant, that I must have fallen asleep over those musty documents."

I trembled as I watched him, waiting for his reply, and I thanked Heaven that in the rôle I had assumed a mask was worn, not only because

184

it hid my features, but because it hid the emotions which these might have betrayed.

"I was beginning to fear," he replied coldly, and without so much as looking at me, "that worse had befallen you."

I breathed again.

"You mean—?"

"Pooh, nothing," said he half contemptuously. "Only methinks 't were well whilst we remain at Canaples that you do not spend your nights in a room within such easy access of the terrace."

"Your advice no doubt is sound, but as I shall not spend another night at Canaples, it comes too late."

"You mean, Monsieur—?"

"That we set out for Paris today."

He shrugged his shoulders.

"Oh, ça! I have just visited the stables, and there are not four horses fit for the journey. So that unless you have in mind the purchase of fresh animals—"

"Pish! My purse is not bottomless," I broke in, repeating the very words that I heard St. Auban utter.

"So you said once before, Monsieur. Still, unless you are prepared to take that course, the only alternative is to remain here until the horses are sufficiently recovered. But perhaps you think of walking?" he added with a sniff.

"Such is your opinion, your time being worthless and it being of little moment where you spend it. I have conceived a plan."

"Ah!"

"Has it not occurred to you that the danger which threatens us and which calls for the protection of a troop is only on this side of the Loire, where the Blaisois might be minded to attempt a rescue of the Chevalier? But over yonder, Chevalier, on the Chambord side, who cares a fig for the Lord of Canaples or his fate? None; is it not so?"

He made an assenting gesture, whereupon I continued:

"This being so, I have bethought me that it will suffice if I take but three or four men and the sergeant as an escort, and cross the river with our prisoner after nightfall, travelling along the opposite shore until we reach Orleans. What think you, Lieutenant?"

He shrugged his shoulders again.

"'T is you who command here," he answered with apathy, "not I."

"Nevertheless, do you not think the plan a safe one, as well as one that will allay his Eminence's very natural impatience?"

"Oh, it is safe enough, I doubt not," he replied coldly.

"Your enthusiasm determines me," quoth I, with an irony that made him wince. "And we will follow the plan, since you agree with me touching its excellence. But keep the matter to yourself until an hour or so after sunset."

He bowed, so utterly my dupe that I could have laughed at him. Then— "There is a little matter that I would mention," he said. "Mademoiselle de Canaples has expressed a wish to accompany her father to Paris and has asked me whether this will be permitted her."

My heart leaped. Surely the gods fought on my side!

"I cannot permit it," I answered icily.

"Monsieur, you are pitiless," he protested in a tone of indignation for which I would gladly have embraced him.

I feigned to ponder.

"The matter needs consideration. Tell Mademoiselle that I will discuss it with her at noon, if she will condescend to await me on the terrace; I will then give her my definite reply. And now, Lieutenant, let us breakfast."

As completely as I had duped Montrésor did I presently dupe those of the troopers with whom I came in contact, among others the sergeant— and anon the Chevalier himself.

From the brief interview that I had with him I discovered that whilst he but vaguely suspected me to be St. Auban—and when I say "he suspected me" I mean he suspected him whose place I had taken— he was, nevertheless, aware of the profit which his captor, whoever he

186

might be, derived from this business. It soon grew clear to me from what he said that St. Auban had mocked him with it whilst concealing his identity; that he had told him how he had obtained from Malpertuis the treasonable letter, and of the bargain which it had enabled him to strike with Mazarin. I did not long remain in his company, and, deeming the time not yet ripe for disclosures, I said little in answer to his lengthy tirades, which had, I guessed, for scope to trap me into betraying the identity he but suspected.

It wanted a few minutes to noon as I left the room in which the old nobleman was confined, and by the door of which a trooper was stationed, musket on shoulder. With every pulse a-throbbing at the thought of my approaching interview with Mademoiselle, I made my way below and out into the bright sunshine, the soldiers I chanced to meet saluting me as I passed them.

On the terrace I found Mademoiselle already awaiting me. She was standing, as often I had seen her stand, with her back turned towards me and her elbows resting upon the balustrade. But as my step sounded behind her, she turned, and stood gazing at me with a face so grief-stricken and pale that I burned to unmask and set her torturing fears at rest. I doffed my hat and greeted her with a silent bow, which she contemptuously disregarded.

"My lieutenant tells me, Mademoiselle," said I in my counterfeited voice, "that it is your desire to bear Monsieur your father company upon this journey of his to Paris."

"With your permission, sir," she answered in a choking voice.

"It is a matter for consideration, Mademoiselle," I pursued. "There are in it many features that may have escaped you, and which I shall discuss with you if you will honour me by stepping into the garden below."

"Why will not the terrace serve?"

"Because I may have that to say which I would not have overheard."

She knit her brows and stared at me as though she would penetrate the black cloth that hid my face. At last she shrugged her shoulders, and letting her arms fall to her side in a gesture of helplessness and resignation—

"Soit; I will go with you," was all she said.

Side by side we went down the steps as a pair of lovers might have gone, save that her face was white and drawn, and that her eyes looked straight before her, and never once, until we reached the gravel path below, at her companion. Side by side we walked along one of the rose-bordered alleys, until at length I stopped.

"Mademoiselle," I said, speaking in the natural tones of that good-for-naught Gaston de Luynes, "I have already decided, and you have my permission to accompany your father."

At the sound of my voice she started, and with her left hand clutching at the region of her heart, she stood, her head thrust forward, and on her face the look of one who is confronted with some awful doubt. That look was brief, however, and swift to replace it was one of hideous revelation.

"In God's name, who are you?" she cried in accents that bespoke internal agony.

"Already you have guessed it, Mademoiselle," I answered, and I would have added that which should have brought comfort to her distraught mind, when—

"You!" she gasped in a voice of profound horror. "You! You, the Judas who has sold my father to the Cardinal for a paltry share in our estates. And I believed that mask of yours to hide the face of St. Auban!"

Her words froze me into a stony mass of insensibility. There was no logic in my attitude; I see it now. Appearances were all against me, and her belief no more than justified. I overlooked all this, and instead of saving time by recounting how I came to be there and thus delivering her from the anguish that was torturing her, I stood, dumb and cruel, cut to the quick by her scorn and her suspicions that I was capable of such a thing as she imputed, and listening to the dictates of an empty pride that prompted me to make her pay full penalty.

"Oh, God pity me!" she wailed. "Have you naught to say?"

Still I maintained my mad, resentful silence. And presently, as one who muses—

"You!" she said again. "You, whom I—" She stopped short. "Oh! The shame of it!" she moaned.

Reason at last came uppermost, and as in my mind I completed her broken sentence, my heart gave a great throb and I was thawed to a gentler purpose.

"Mademoiselle!" I exclaimed.

But even as I spoke, she turned, and sweeping aside her gown that it might not touch me, she moved rapidly towards the steps we had just descended. Full of remorse, I sprang after her.

"Mademoiselle! Hear me," I cried, and put forth my hand to stay her. Thereat she wheeled round and faced me, a blaze of fury in her grey eyes.

"Dare not to touch me," she panted. "You thief, you hound!"

I recoiled, and, like one turned to stone, I stood and watched her mount the steps, my feelings swaying violently between anger and sorrow. Then my eye fell upon Montrésor standing on the topmost step, and on his face there was a sneering, insolent smile which told me that he had heard the epithets she had bestowed upon me.

Albeit I sought that day another interview with Yvonne, I did not gain it, and so I was forced to sun myself in solitude upon the terrace. But I cherished for my consolation that broken sentence of hers, whereby I read that the coldness which she had evinced for me before I left Canaples had only been assumed.

And presently as I recalled what talks we had had, and one in particular from which it now appeared to me that her coldness had sprung, a light seemed suddenly to break upon my mind, as perchance it hath long ago broken upon the minds of those who may happen upon these pages, and whose wits in matters amorous are of a keener temper than were mine.

I who in all things had been arrogant, presumptuous, and self-satisfied, had methought erred for once through over-humility.

And, indeed, even as I sat and pondered on that June day, it seemed to me a thing incredible that she whom I accounted the most queenly and superb of women should have deigned to grant a tender thought to one so mean, so far beneath her as I had ever held myself to be.

CHAPTER XXVI

REPARATION

Things came to pass that night as I had planned, and the fates which of late had smiled upon me were kind unto the end.

Soon after ten, and before the moon had risen, a silent procession wended its way from the château to the river. First went Montrésor and two of his men; next came the Chevalier with Mademoiselle, and on either side of them a trooper; whilst I, in head-piece and back and breast of steel, went last with Mathurin, the sergeant—who warmly praised the plan I had devised for the conveyance of M. de Canaples to Paris without further loss of time.

Two boats which I had caused to be secretly procured were in readiness, and by these a couple of soldiers awaited us, holding the bridles of eight horses, one of which was equipped with a lady's saddle. Five of these belonged—or had belonged—to the Chevalier, whilst the others were three of those that had brought the troop from Paris, and which I, in the teeth of all protestations, had adjudged sufficiently recovered for the return journey.

The embarkation was safely effected, M. de Canaples and Mademoiselle in one boat with Montrésor, Mathurin, and myself; the sergeant took the oars; Montrésor and I kept watch over our prisoner. In the other boat came the four troopers, who were to accompany us, and one other who was to take the boats, and Montrésor in them, back to Canaples. For the lieutenant was returning, so that he might, with the remainder of the troop, follow us to Paris so soon as the condition of the horses would permit it.

The beasts we took with us were swimming the stream, guided and upheld by the men in the other boat.

Just as the moon began to show her face our bow grated on the shore at the very point where I had intended that we should land. I sprang out and turned to assist Mademoiselle.

But, disdaining my proffered hand, she stepped ashore unaided. The Chevalier came next, and after him Montrésor and Mathurin.

Awhile we waited until the troopers brought their boat to land, then when they had got the snorting animals safely ashore, I bade them look to the prisoner, and requested Montrésor and Mathurin to step aside with me, as I had something to communicate to them.

Walking between the pair, I drew them some twenty paces away from the group by the water, towards a certain thicket in which I had bidden Michelot await me.

"It has occurred to me, Messieurs," I began, speaking slowly and deliberately as we paced along,—"it has occurred to me that despite all the precautions taken to carry out my Lord Cardinal's wishes—a work at least in which you, yourselves, have evinced a degree of zeal that I cannot too highly commend to his Eminence—the possibility yet remains of some mistake of trivial appearance, of some slight flaw that might yet cause the miscarriage of those wishes."

They turned towards me, and although I could not make out the expressions of their faces, in the gloom, yet I doubted not but that they were puzzled ones at that lengthy and apparently meaningless harangue.

The sergeant was the first to speak, albeit I am certain that he understood the less.

"I venture, M. le Capitaine, to think that your fears, though very natural, are groundless."

"Say you so?" quoth I, with a backward glance to assure myself that we were screened by the trees from the eyes of those behind us. "Say you so? Well, well, mayhap you are right, though you speak of my fears being groundless. I alluded to some possible mistake of yours—yours and M. de Montrésor's—not of mine. And, by Heaven, a monstrous flaw there is in this business, for if either of you so much as whisper I'll blow your brains out!"

And to emphasise these words, as sinister as they were unlooked-for, I raised both hands suddenly from beneath my cloak, and clapped the cold nose of a pistol to the head of each of them.

I was obeyed as men are obeyed who thus uncompromisingly prove the force of their commands. Seeing them resigned, I whistled softly, and in answer there was a rustle from among the neighbouring trees, and presently two shadows emerged from the thicket. In less time than it takes me to relate it, Montrésor and his sergeant found themselves gagged, and each securely bound to a tree.

Then, with Michelot and Abdon following a short distance behind me, I made my way back to the troopers, and, feigning to stumble as I approached, I hurtled so violently against two of them that I knocked the pair headlong into the stream.

Scarce was it done, and almost before the remaining three had realised it, there was a pistol at the head of each of them and sweet promises of an eternal hereafter being whispered in their ears. They bore themselves with charming discretion, and like lambs we led them each to a tree and dealt with them as we had dealt with their officers, whilst the Chevalier and his daughter watched us, bewildered and dumfounded at what they saw.

As soon as the other two had crawled—all unconscious of the fates of their comrades—out of the river, we served them also in a like manner.

Bidding Abdon and Michelot lead the horses, and still speaking in my assumed voice, I desired Mademoiselle and the Chevalier—who had not yet sufficiently recovered from his bewilderment to have found his tongue—to follow me. I led the way up the gentle slope to the spot where our first victims were pinioned.

Montrésor's comely young face looked monstrous wicked in the moonlight, and his eyes rolled curiously as he beheld me. Stepping up to him I freed him of his gag—an act which I had almost regretted a moment later, for he cleared his throat with so lusty a torrent of profanity that methought the heavens must have fallen on us. At last when he was done with that—"Before you leave me in this plight, M. de St. Auban," quoth he, "perchance you will satisfy me with an explanation of your unfathomable deeds and of this violence."

"St. Auban!" exclaimed the Chevalier.

"St. Auban!" cried Yvonne.

And albeit wonder rang in both their voices, yet their minds I knew went different ways.

"No, not St. Auban," I answered with a laugh and putting aside all counterfeit of speech.

"Par la mort Dieu! I know that voice," cried Montrésor.

"Mayhap, indeed! And know you not this face?" And as I spoke I whipped away my wig and mask, and thrust my countenance close up to his.

"Thunder of God!" ejaculated the boy. Then—"Pardieu," he added, "there is Michelot! How came I not to recognise him?"

"Since you would not assist me, Montrésor, you see I was forced to do without you."

"But St. Auban?" he gasped. "Where is he?"

"In heaven, I hope—but I doubt it sadly."

"You have killed him?"

There and then, as briefly as I might, I told him, whilst the others stood by to listen, how I had come upon the Marquis in the château the night before and what had passed thereafter.

"And now," I said, as I cut his bonds, "it grieves me to charge you with an impolite errand to his Eminence, but—"

"I'll not return to him," he burst out. "I dare not. Mon Dieu, you have ruined me, Luynes!"

194

"Then come with me, and I'll build your fortunes anew and on a sounder foundation. I have an influential letter in my pocket that should procure us fortune in the service of the King of Spain."

He needed little pressing to fall in with my invitation, so we set the sergeant free, and him instead I charged with a message that must have given Mazarin endless pleasure when it was delivered to him. But he had the Canaples estates wherewith to console himself and his never-failing maxim that "chi canta, paga." Touching the Canaples estates, however, he did not long enjoy them, for when he went into exile, two years later, the Parliament returned them to their rightful owner.

The Chevalier de Canaples approached me timidly.

"Monsieur," quoth he, "I have wronged you very deeply. And this generous rescue of one who has so little merited your aid truly puts me to so much shame that I know not what thanks to offer you."

"Then offer none, Monsieur," I answered, taking his proffered hand. "Moreover, time presses and we have a possible pursuit to baffle. So to horse, Monsieurs."

I assisted Mademoiselle to mount, and she passively suffered me to do her this office, having no word for me, and keeping her face averted from my earnest gaze.

I sighed as I turned to mount the horse Michelot held for me; but methinks 't was more a sigh of satisfaction than of pain.

. . . . .

All that night we travelled and all next day until Tours was reached towards evening. There we halted for a sorely needed rest and for fresh horses.

Three days later we arrived at Nantes, and a week from the night of the Chevalier's rescue we took ship from that port to Santander.

That same evening, as I leaned upon the taffrail watching the distant coast line of my beloved France, whose soil meseemed I was not like to tread again for years, Yvonne came softly up behind me.

"Monsieur," she said in a voice that trembled somewhat, "I have, indeed, misjudged you. The shame of it has made me hold aloof from you since we left Blois. I cannot tell you, Monsieur, how deep that shame has been, or with what sorrow I have been beset for the words I uttered at Canaples. Had I but paused to think——"

"Nay, nay, Mademoiselle, 't was all my fault, I swear. I left you overlong the dupe of appearances."

"But I should not have believed them so easily. Say that I am forgiven, Monsieur," she pleaded; "tell me what reparation I can make."

"There is one reparation that you can make if you are so minded," I answered, "but 'tis a life-long reparation."

They were bold words, indeed, but my voice played the coward and shook so vilely that it bereft them of half their boldness. But, ah, Dieu, what joy, what ecstasy was mine to see how they were read by her; to remark the rich, warm blood dyeing her cheeks in a bewitching blush; to behold the sparkle that brightened her matchless eyes as they met mine!

"Yvonne!"

"Gaston!"

She was in my arms at last, and the work of reparation was begun whilst together we gazed across the sun-gilt sea towards the fading shores of France.

If you be curious to learn how, guided by the gentle hand of her who plucked me from the vile ways that in my old life I had trodden, I have since achieved greatness, honour, and renown, History will tell you.

Ingram Content Group UK Ltd.
Milton Keynes UK
UKHW020132050723
424569UK00005B/114